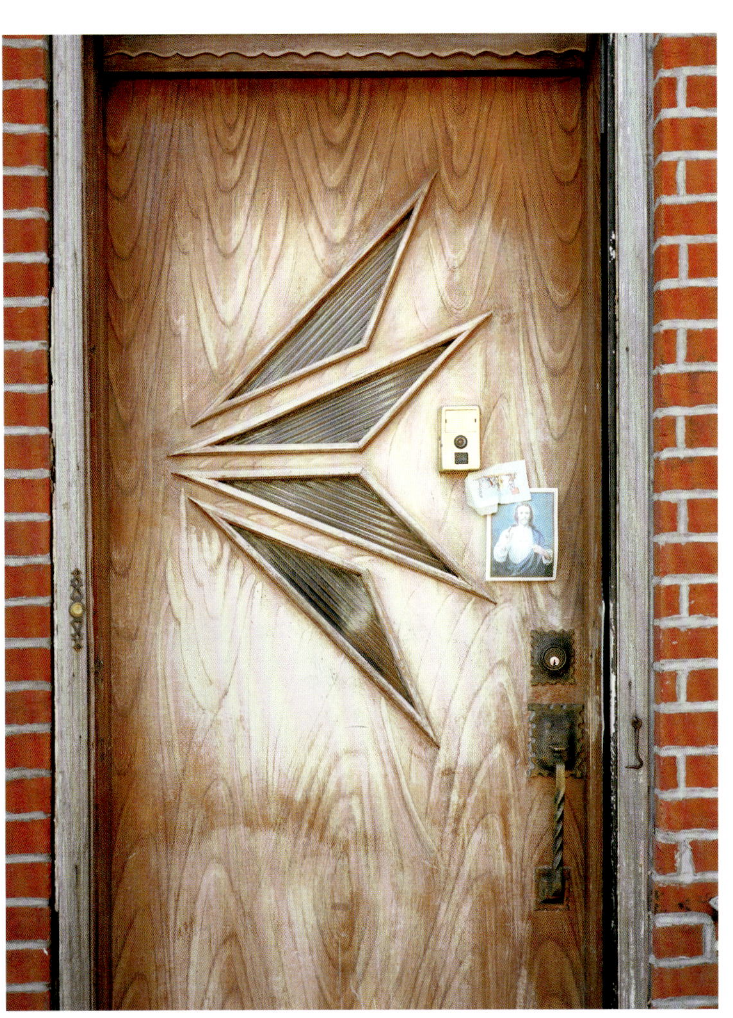

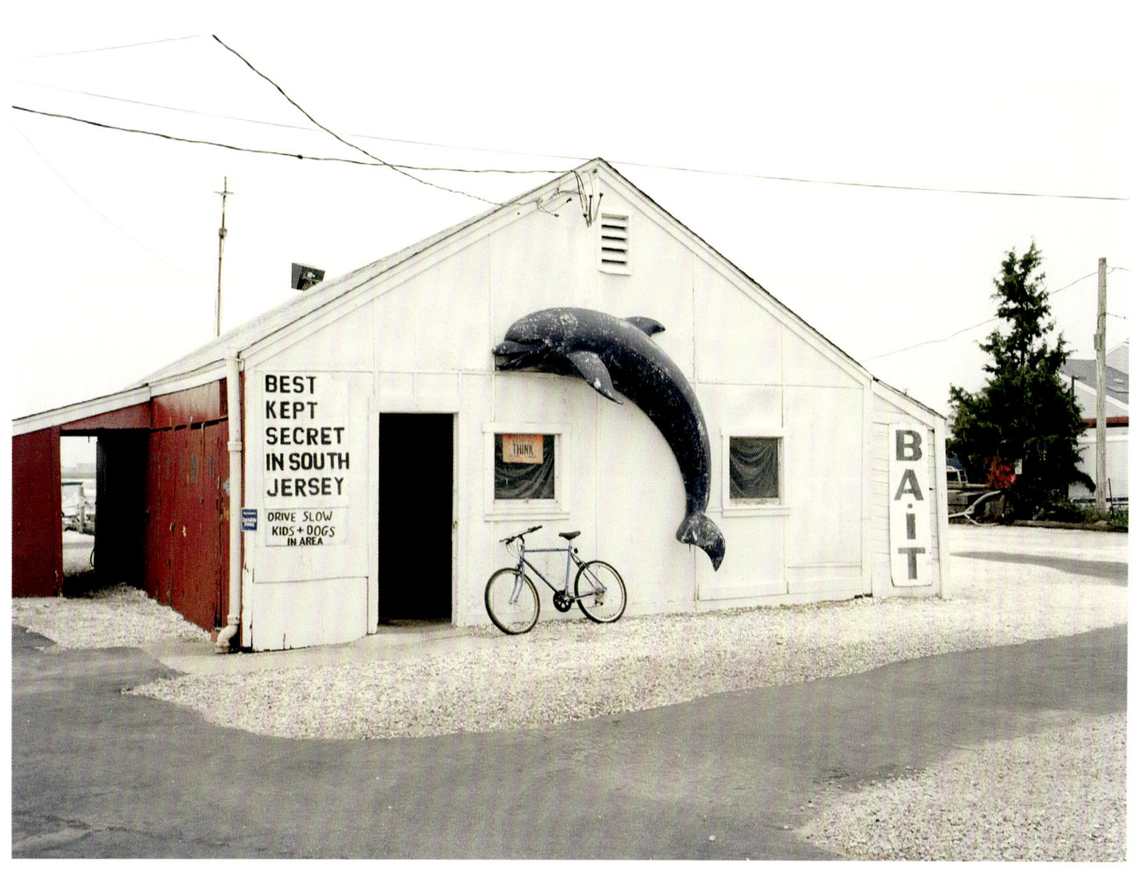

BEST
KEPT
SECRET
IN SOUTH
JERSEY
DRIVE SLOW
KIDS + DOGS
IN AREA
THINK
BAiT

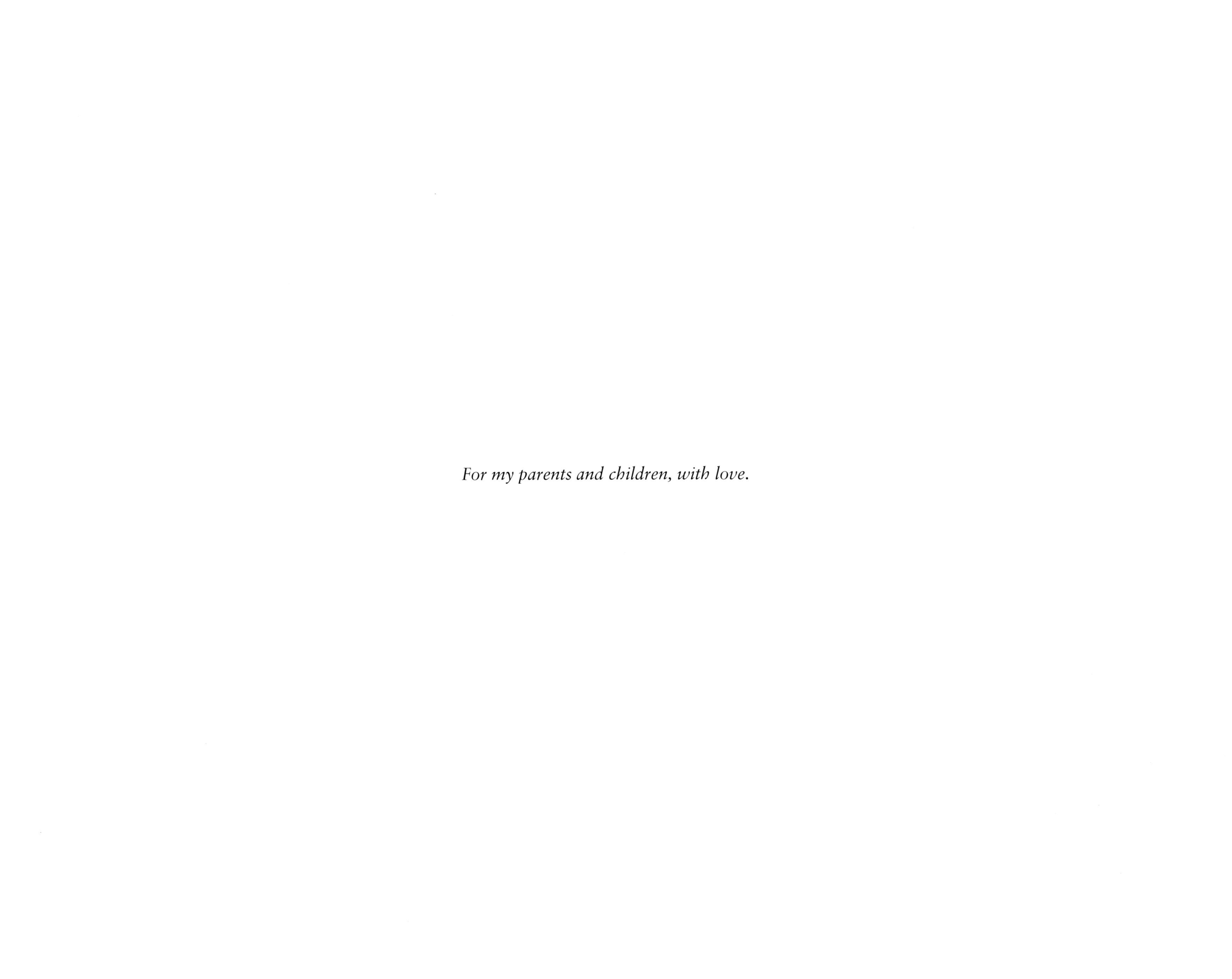

For my parents and children, with love.

Cofounders: Taj Forer and Michael Itkoff
Creative Director: Ursula Damm
Copy Editor: Gabrielle Fastman

ISBN: 978-1-954119-05-5

Printed by Ofset Yapimevi, Turkey

Daylight Books
E-mail: info@daylightbooks.org
Web: www.daylightbooks.org

Martin Buday

PROPHETIC KINGDOM

Daylight

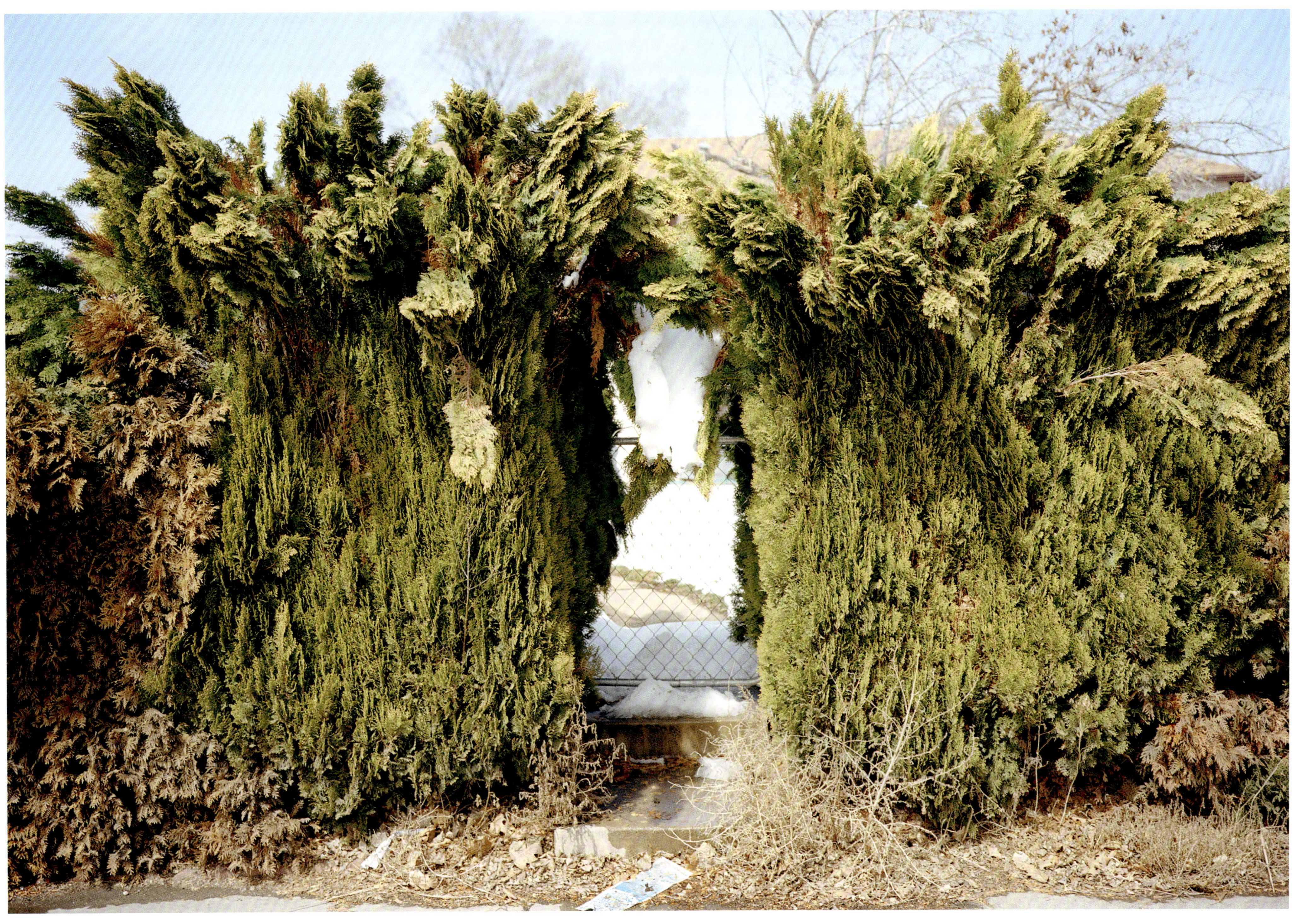

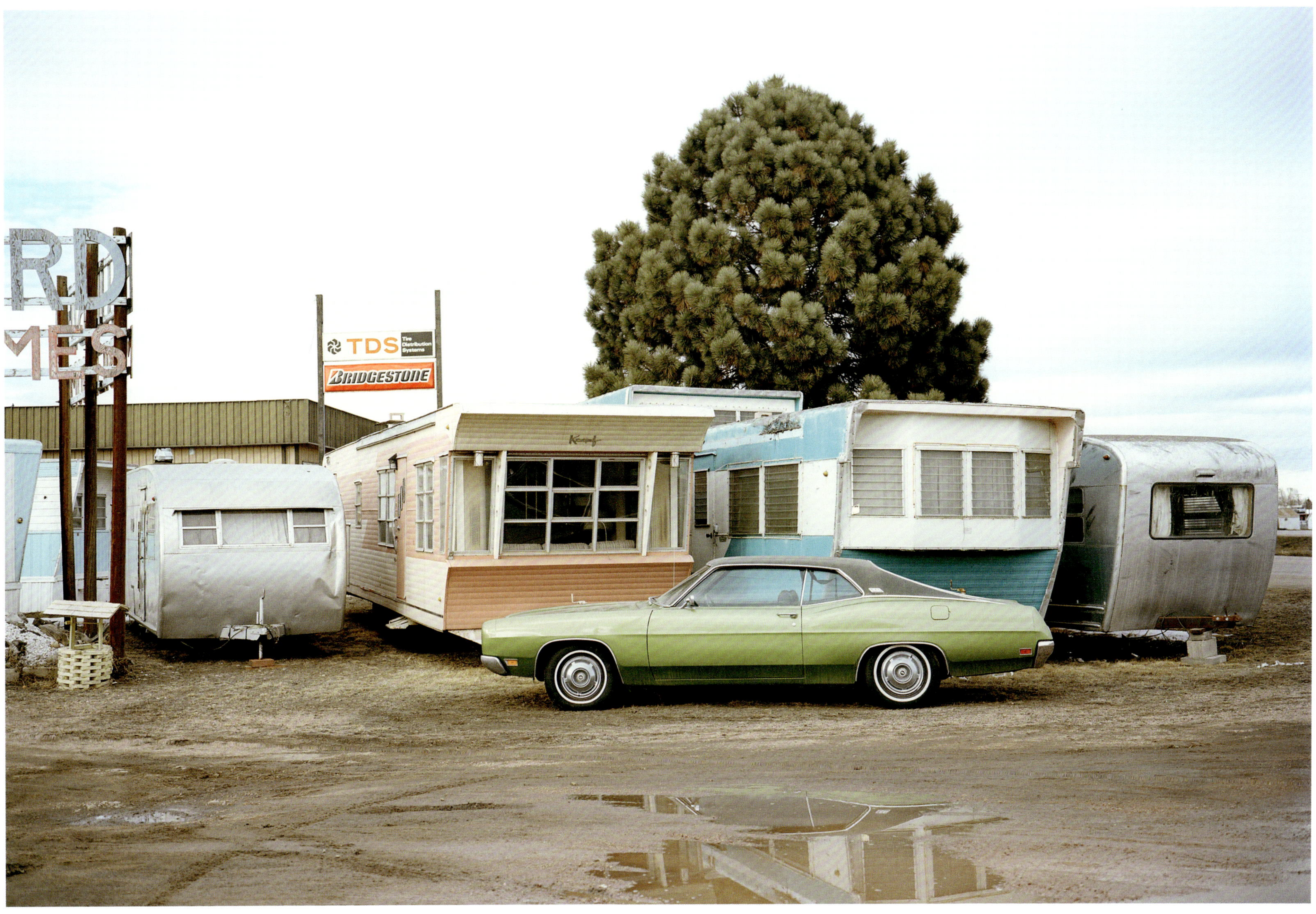

RD
MES
TDS Tire Distribution Systems
BRIDGESTONE

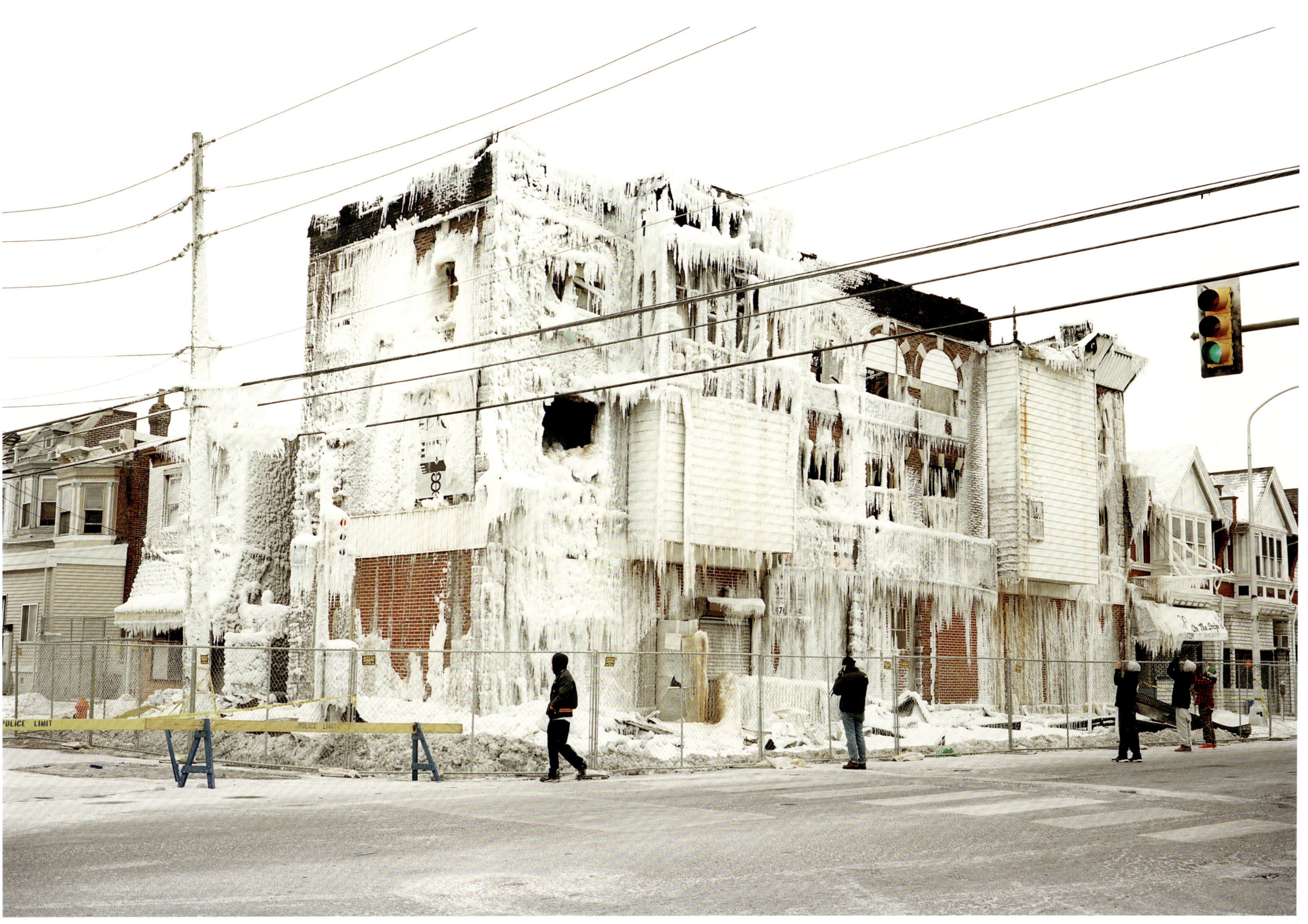

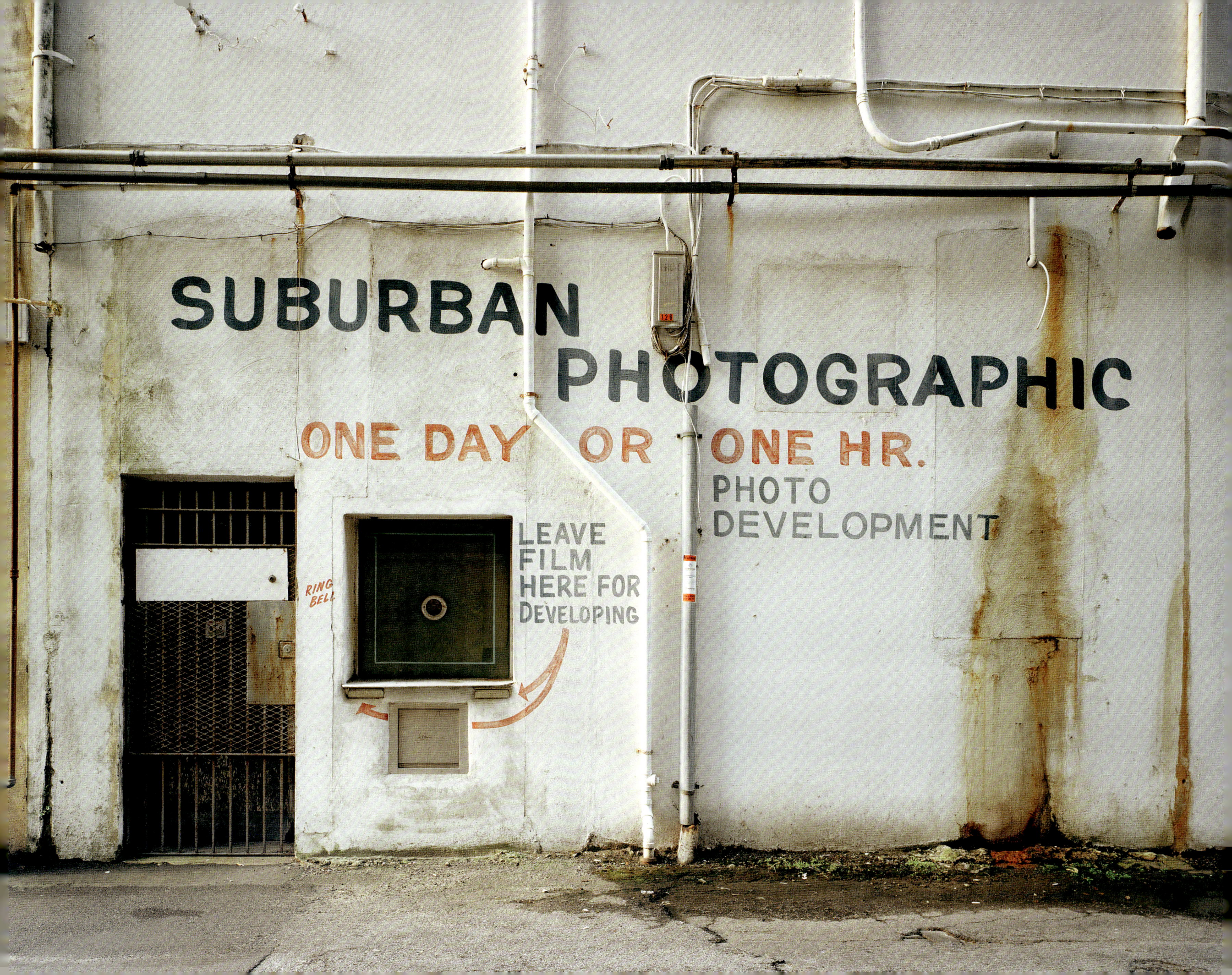

SUBURBAN
PHOTOGRAPHIC
ONE DAY OR ONE HR.
PHOTO
DEVELOPMENT
LEAVE
FILM
HERE FOR
Developing
RING
BELL

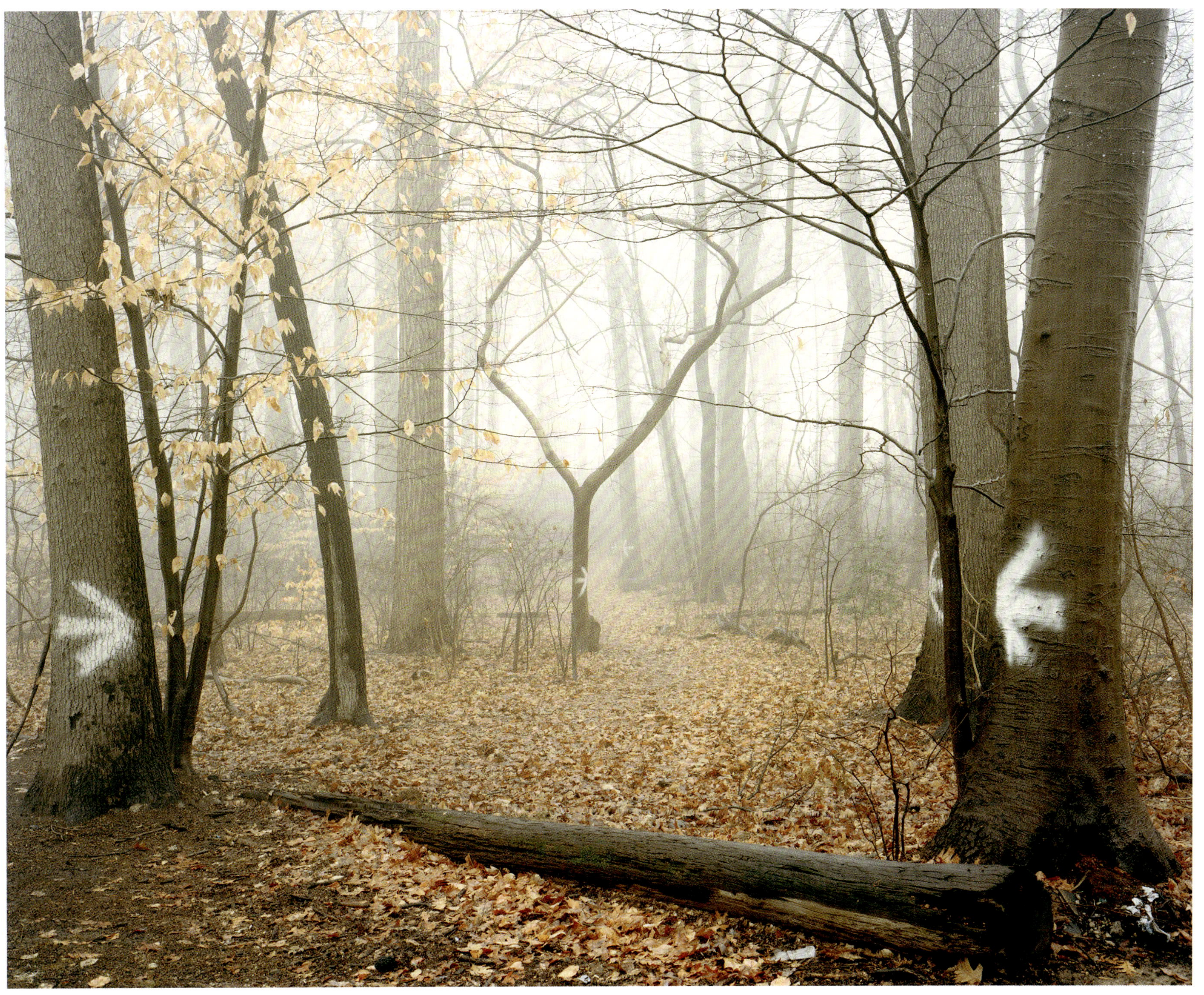

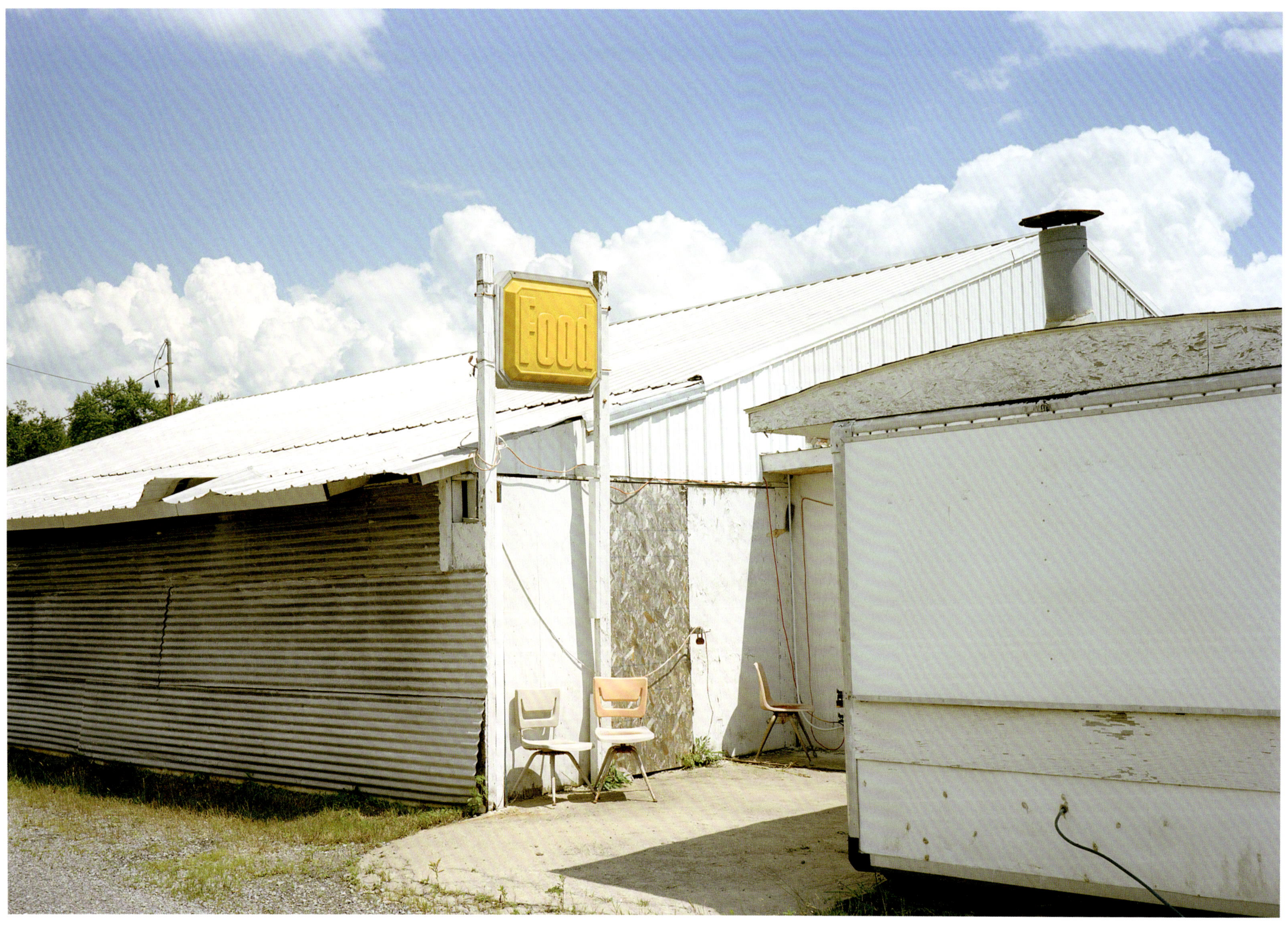
Food

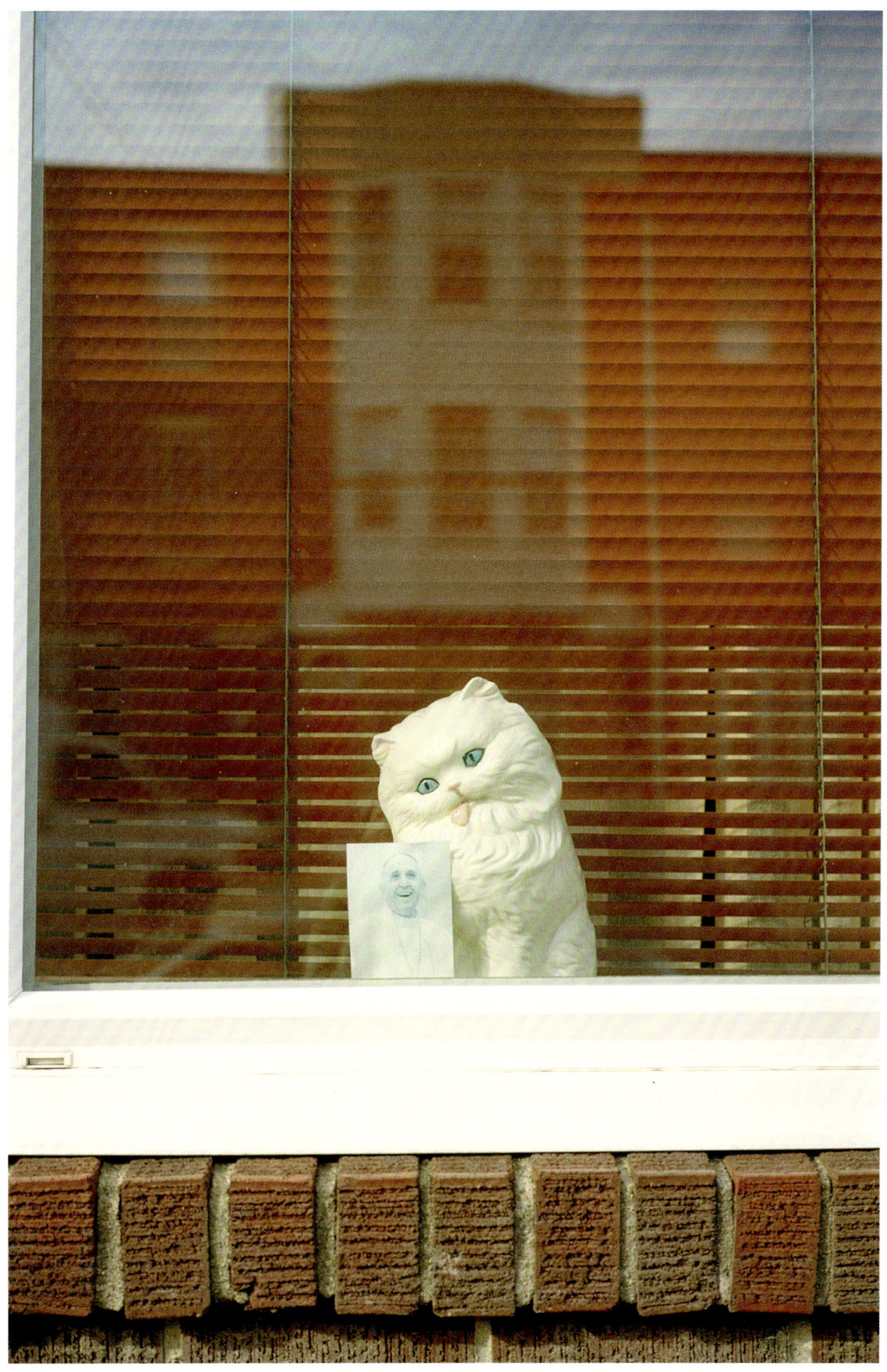

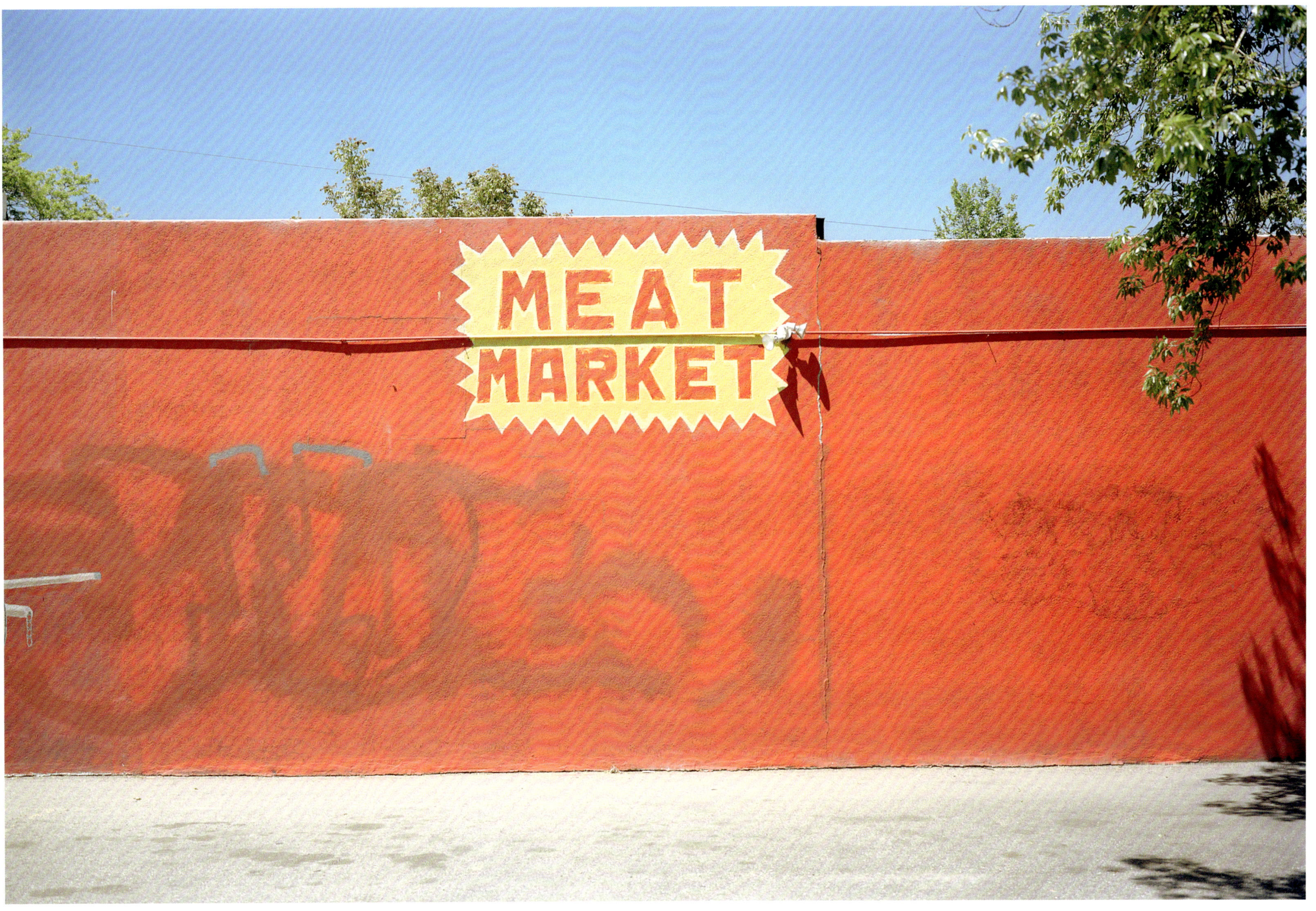

MEAT
MARKET

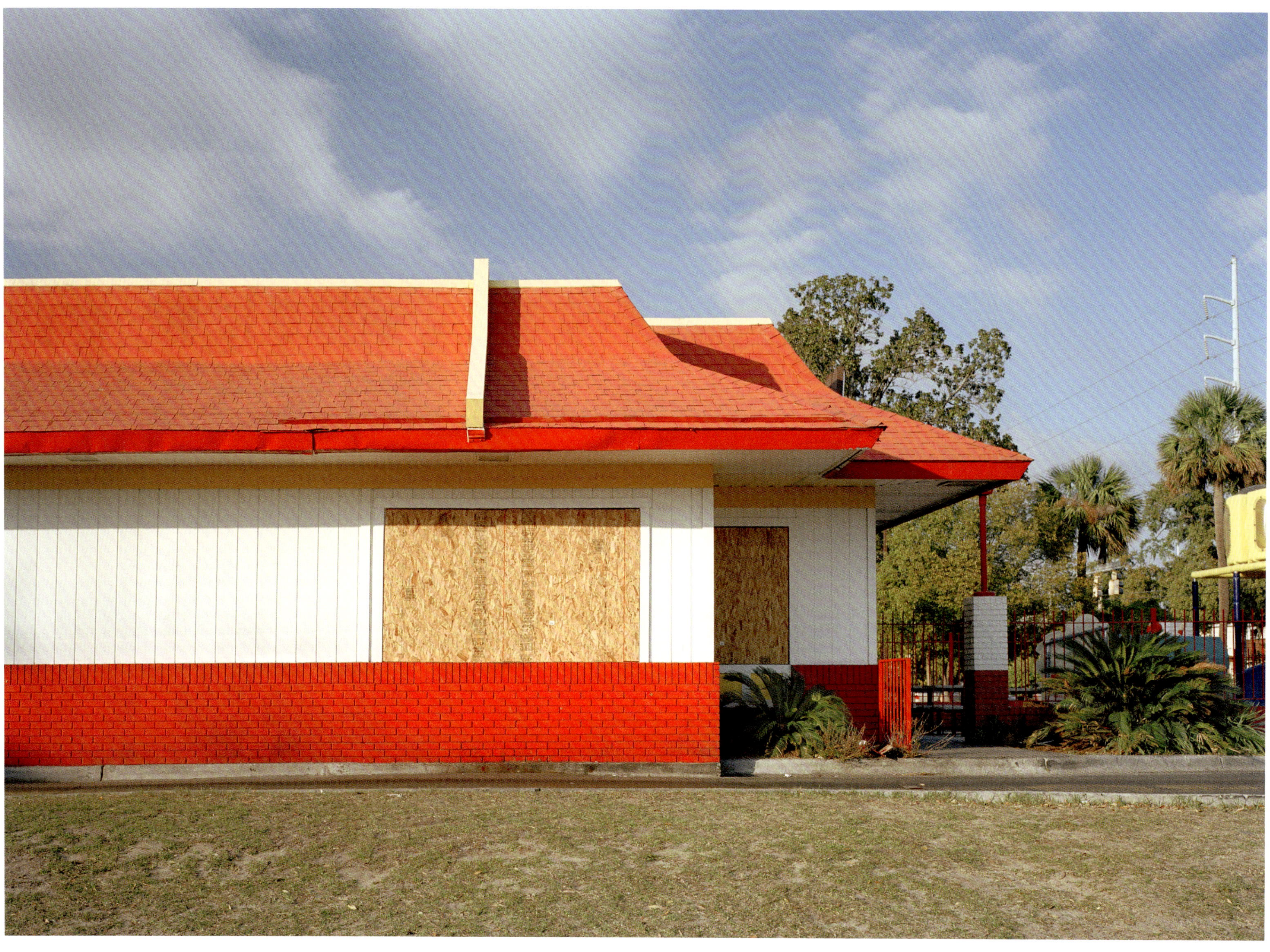

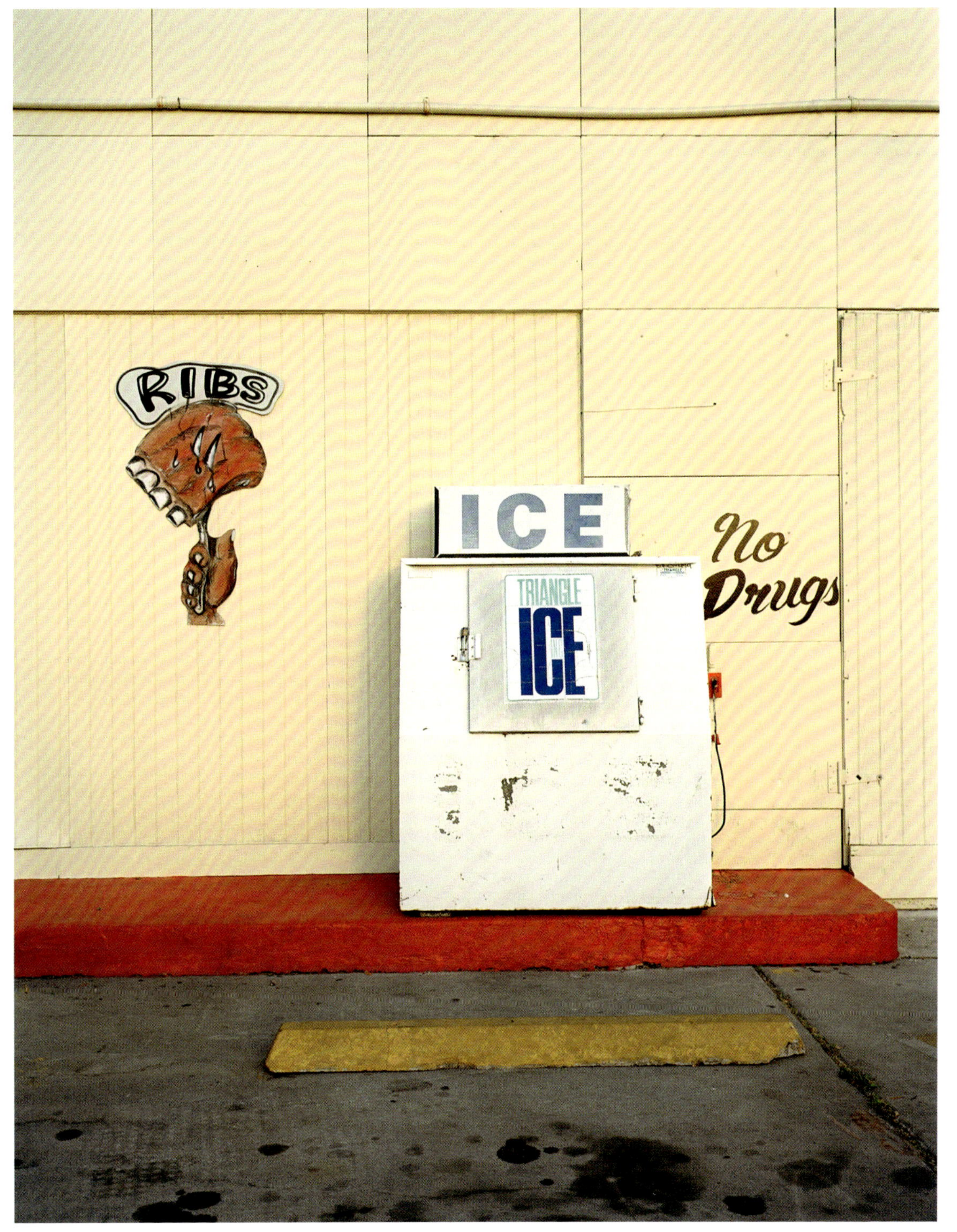
RIBS
ICE
TRIANGLE
ICE
No
Drugs

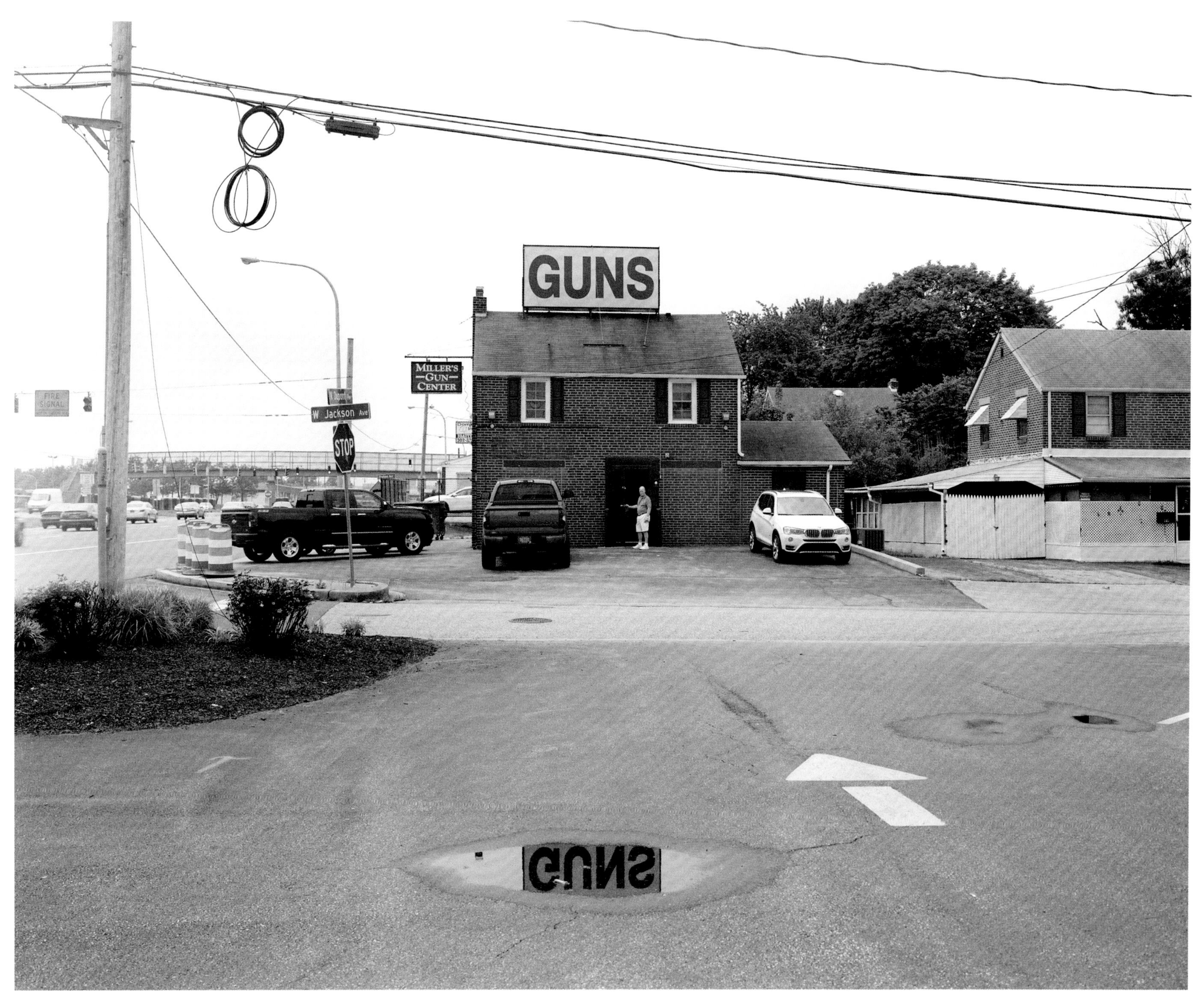

GUNS
MILLER'S
GUN
CENTER
FIRE
SIGNAL
W Jackson Ave
STOP
GUNS

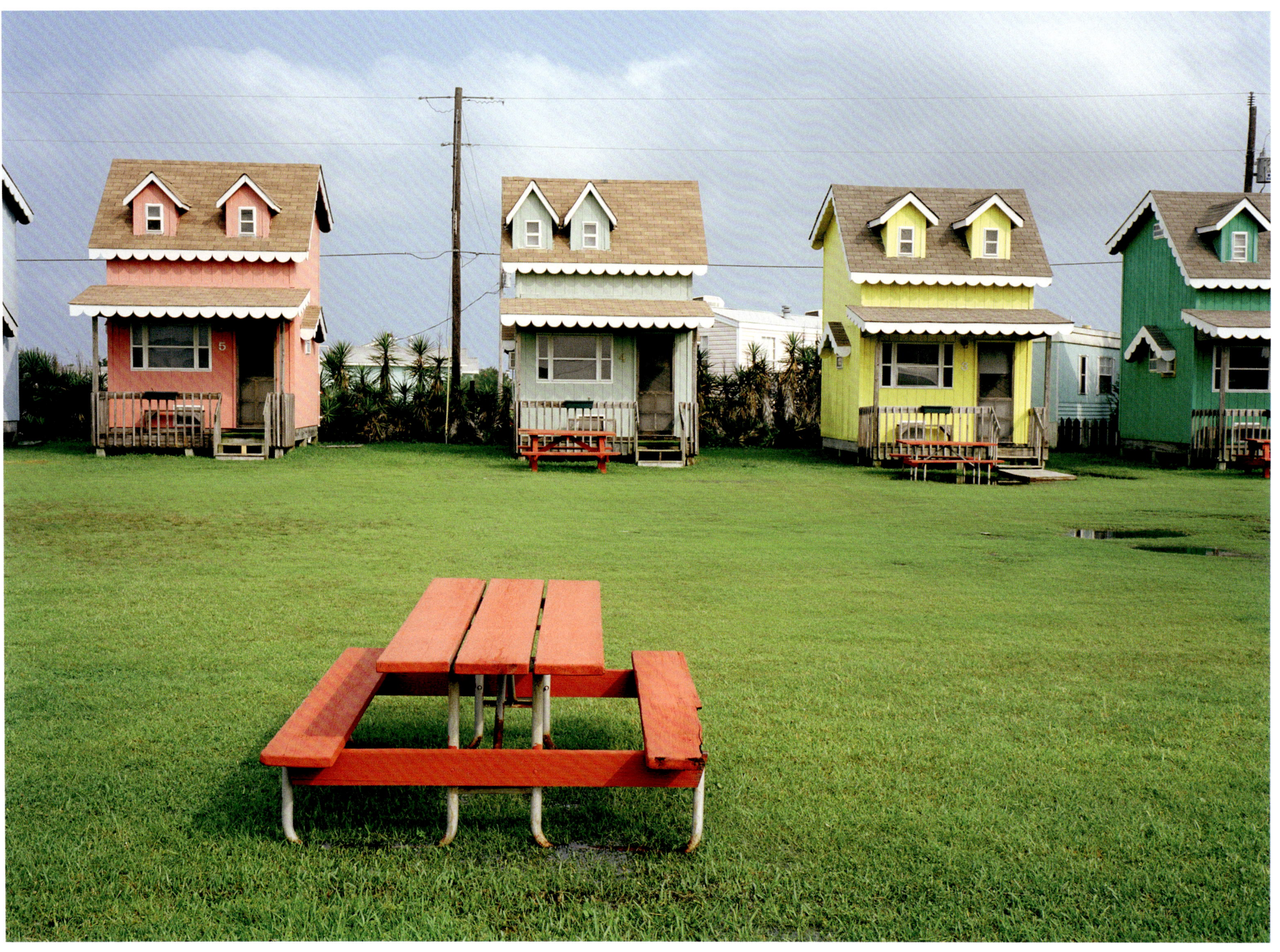

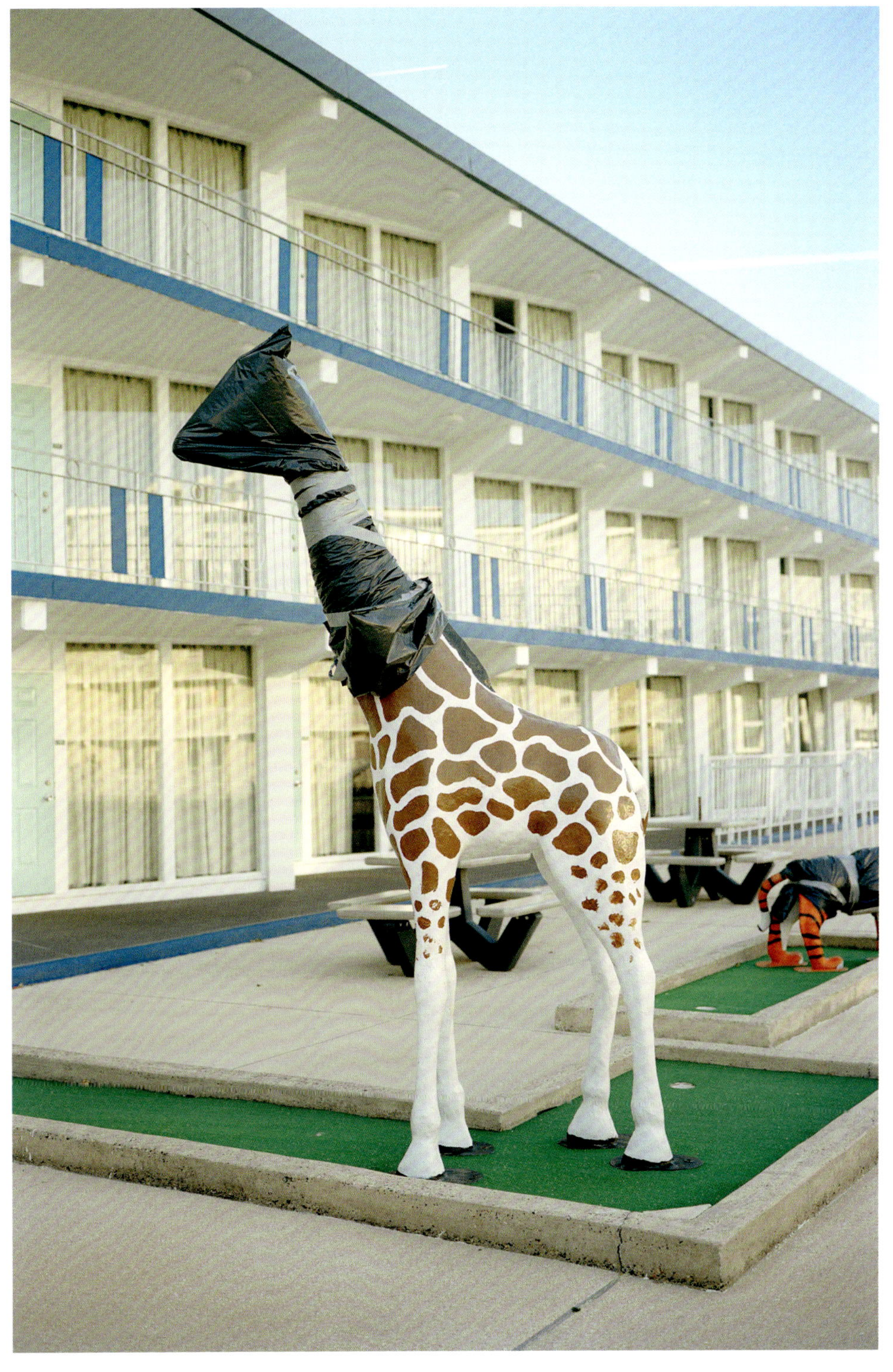

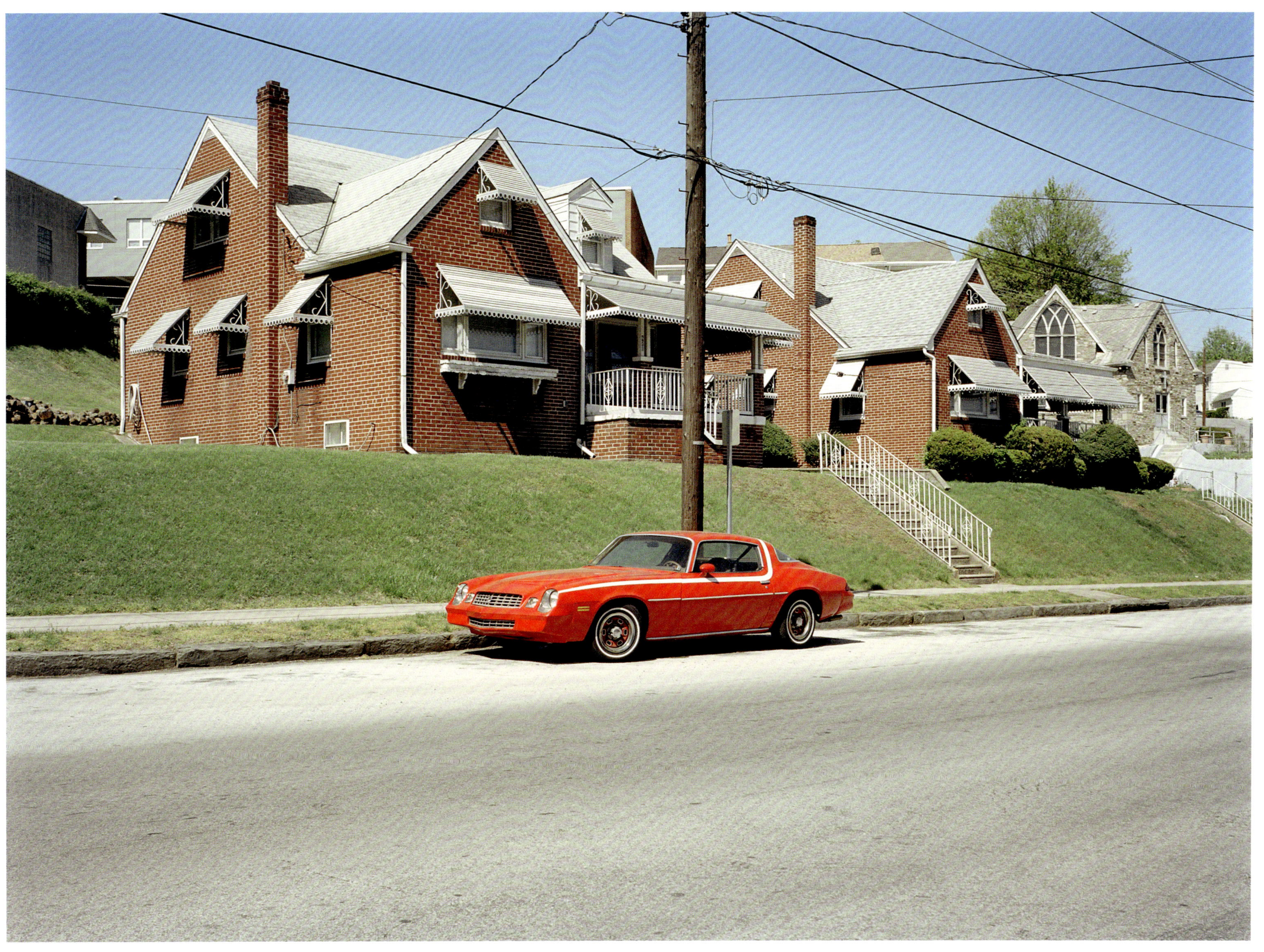

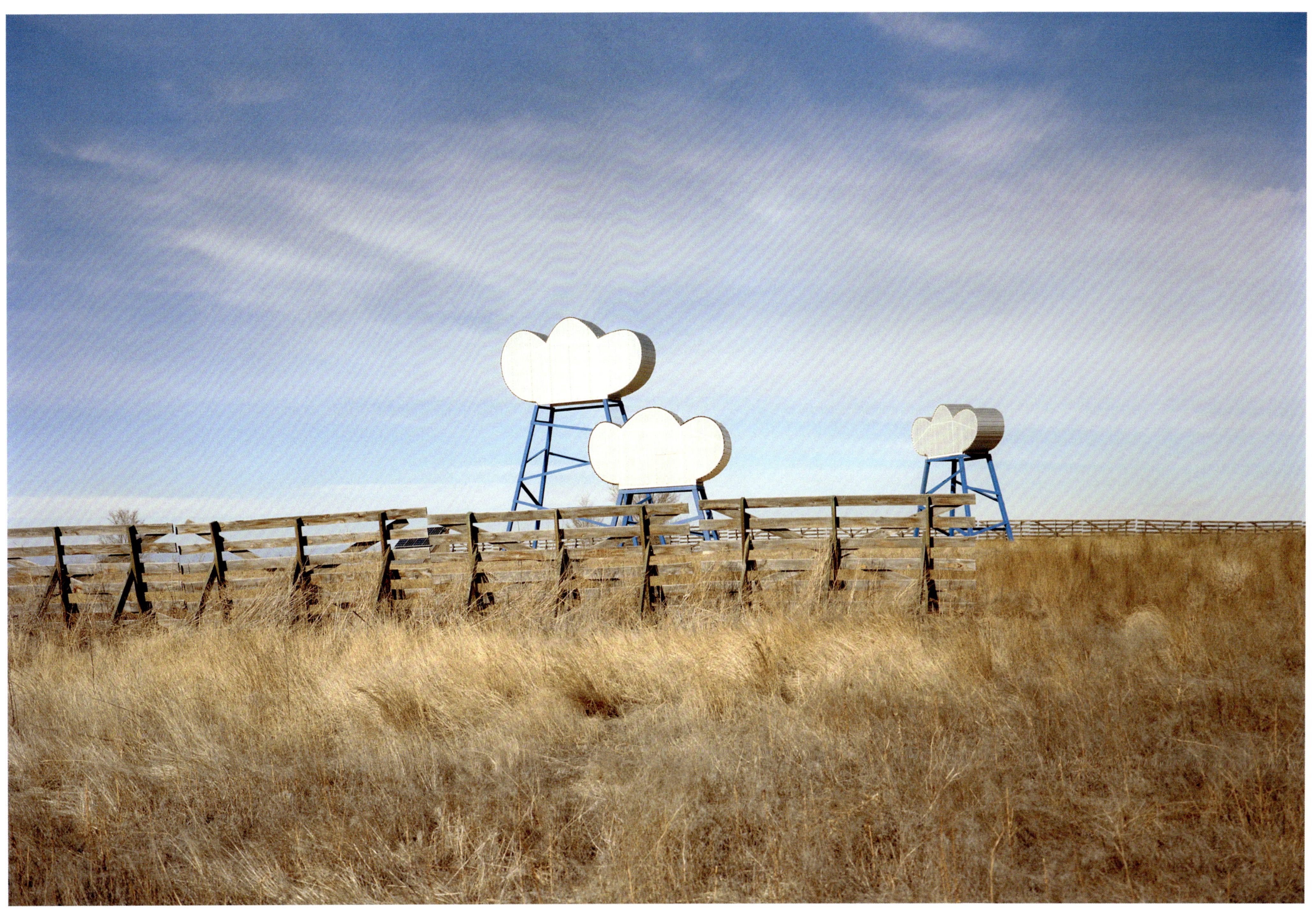

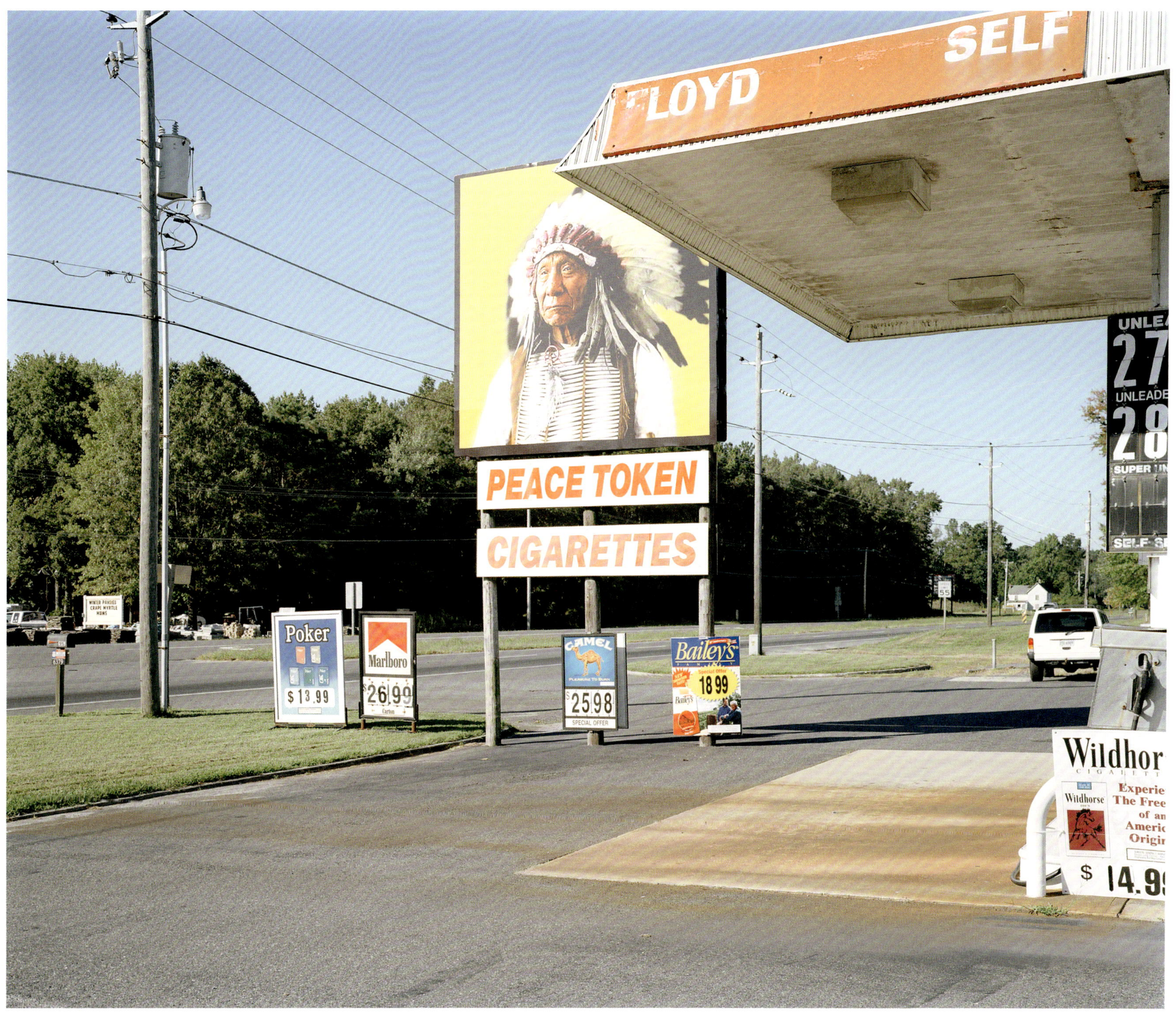
LOYD
SELF
PEACE TOKEN
CIGARETTES
UNLE
27
UNLEADE
28
SUPER UN
SELF S
Poker
Marlboro
$13.99
26.99
Carton
CAMEL
PLEASURE TO BURN
25.98
SPECIAL OFFER
Bailey's
Special Offer
18.99
Bailey's
Wildhor
CIGARETT
Wildhorse
Experie
The Free
of an
Americ
Origin
$14.99

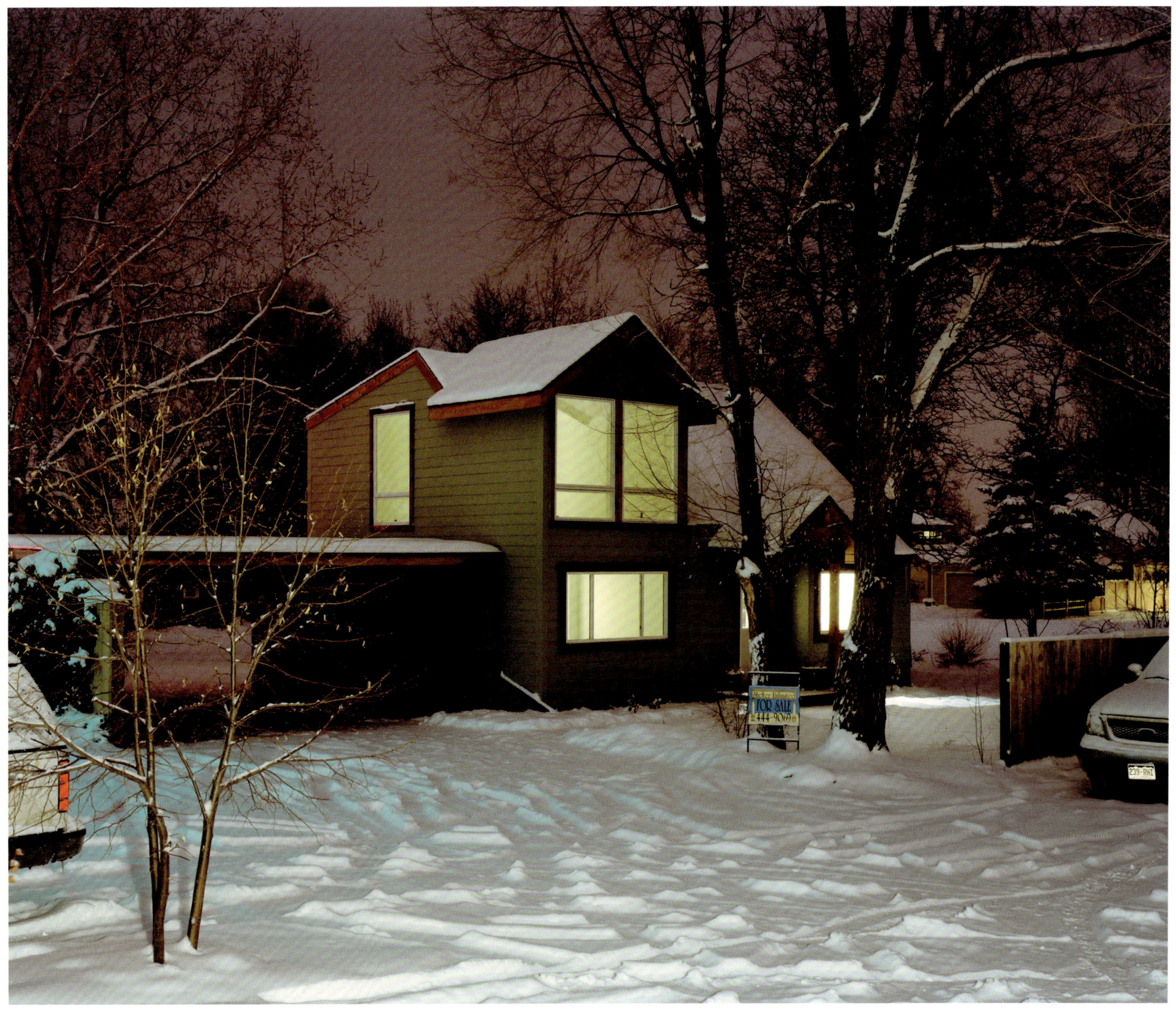
FOR SALE
444-9069

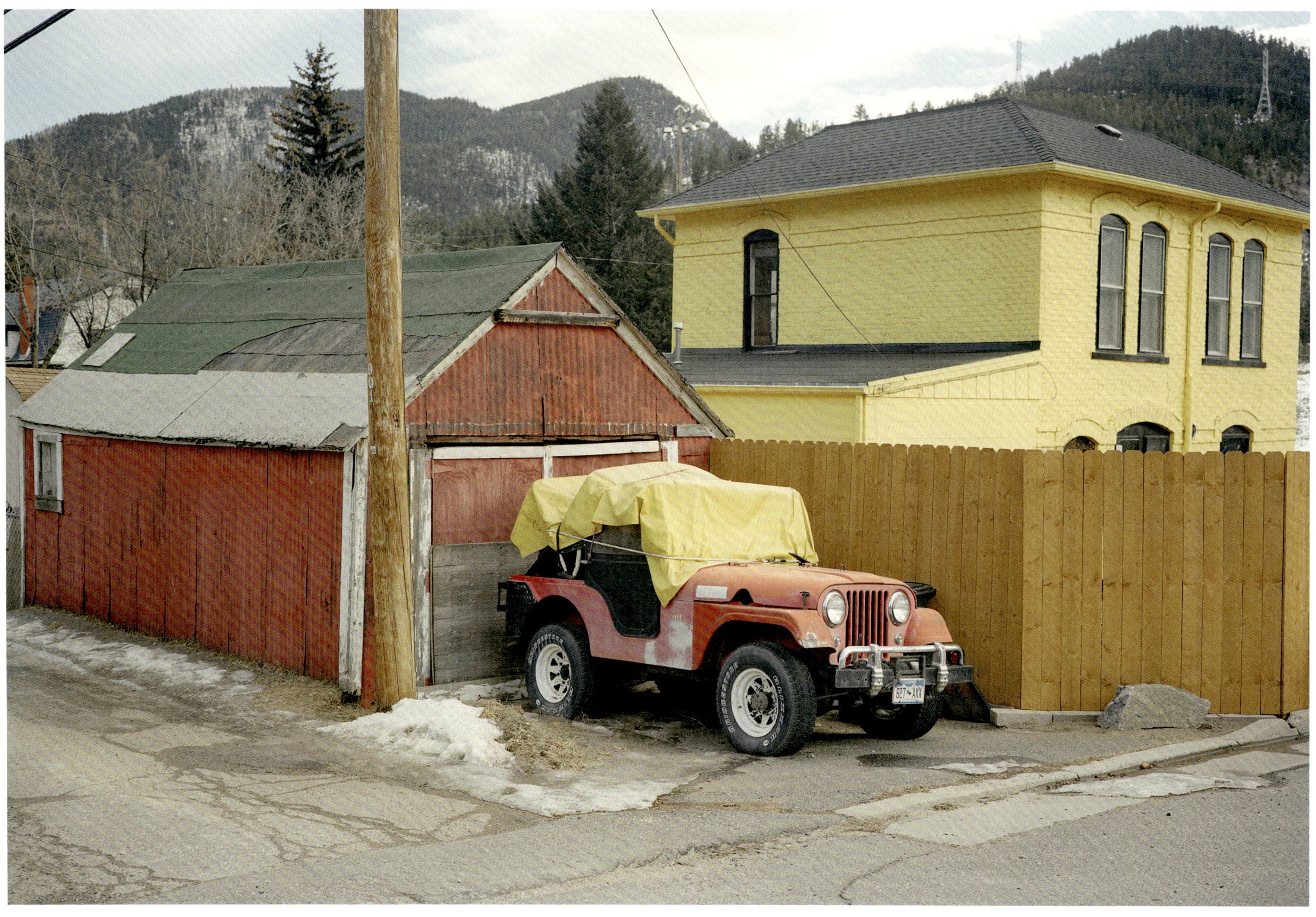

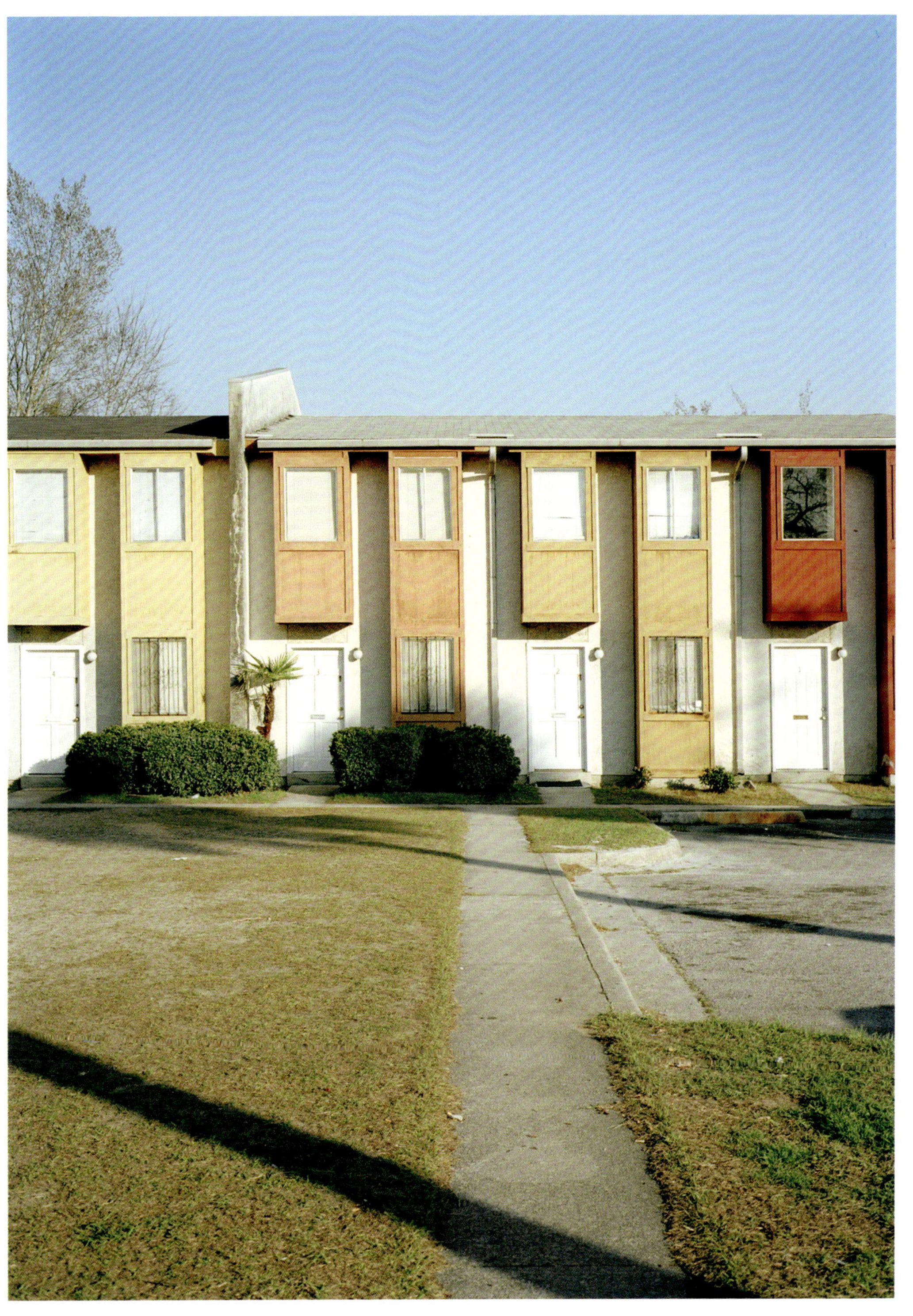

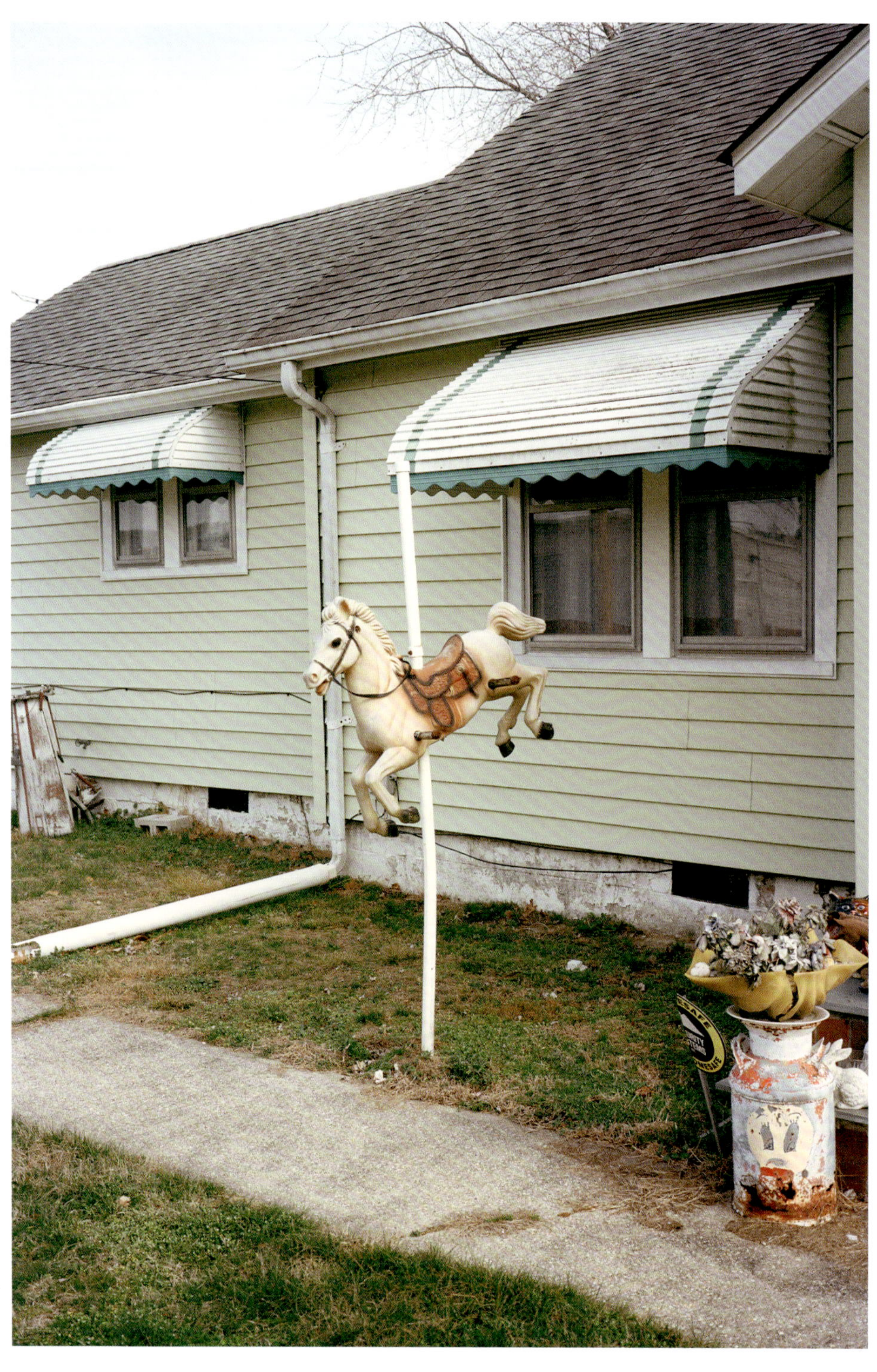

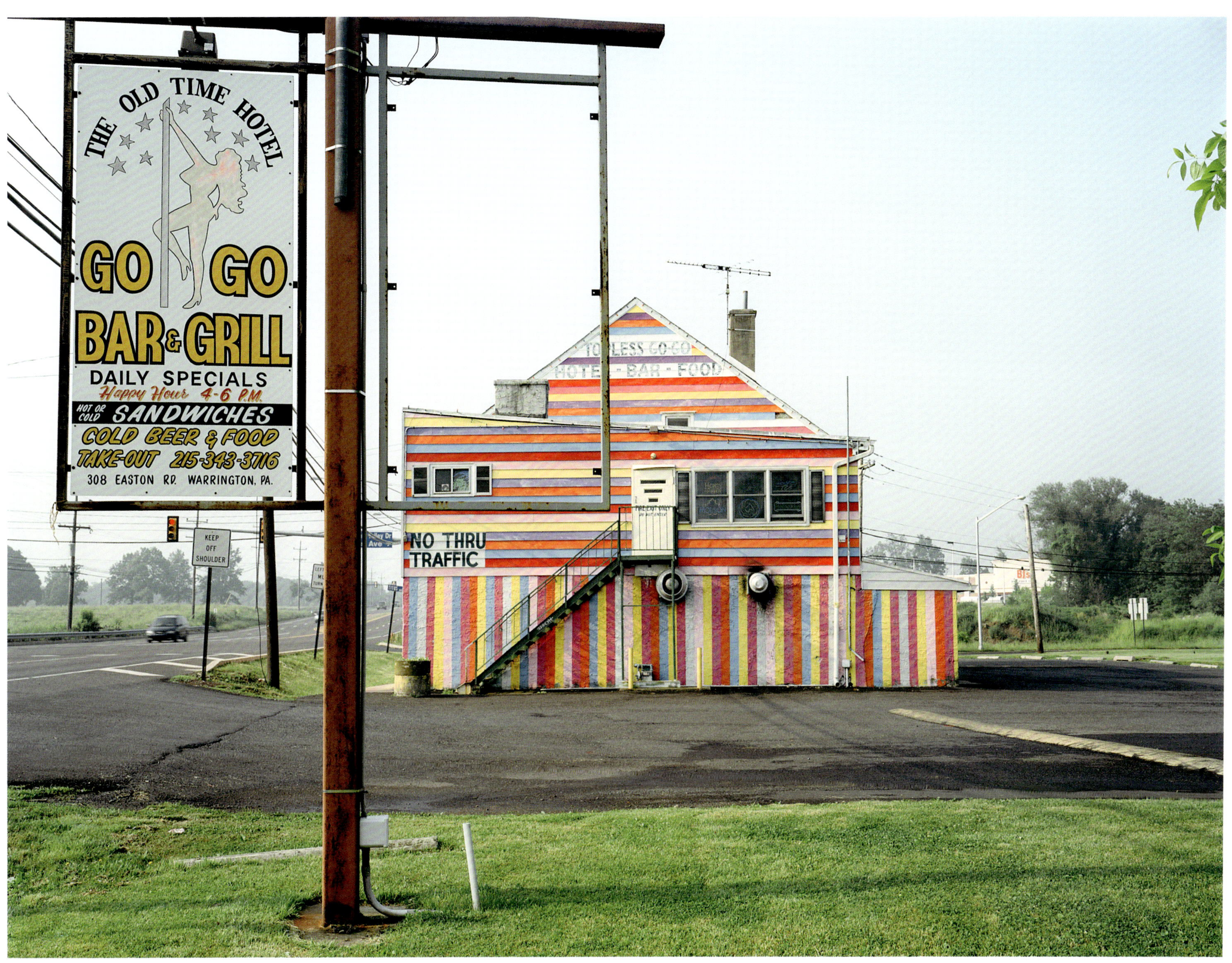

THE OLD TIME HOTEL
GO GO
BAR & GRILL
DAILY SPECIALS
Happy Hour 4-6 P.M.
HOT OR COLD SANDWICHES
COLD BEER & FOOD
TAKE-OUT 215-343-3716
308 EASTON RD. WARRINGTON, PA.
TOPLESS GO-GO
HOTEL - BAR - FOOD
NO THRU TRAFFIC
KEEP OFF SHOULDER

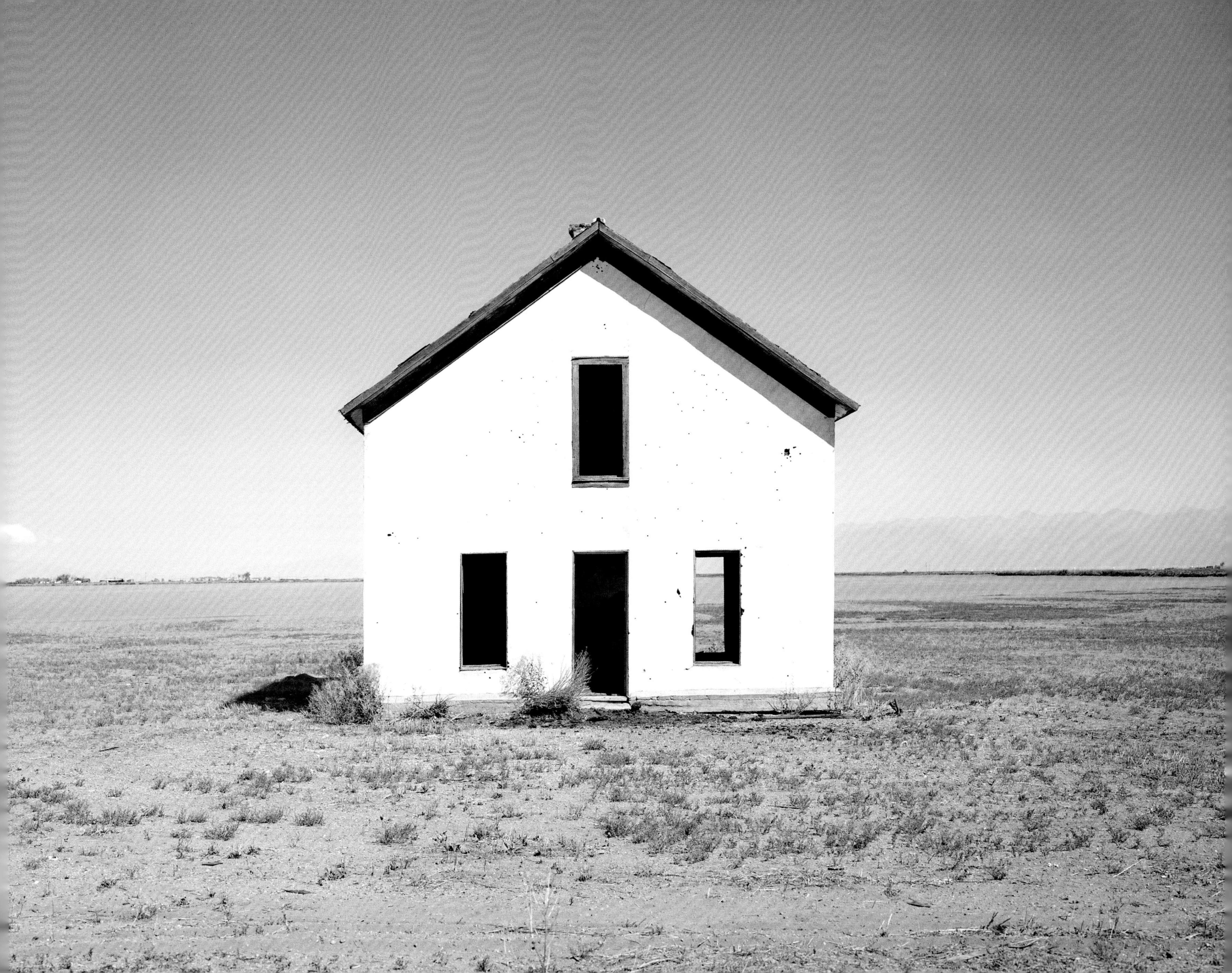

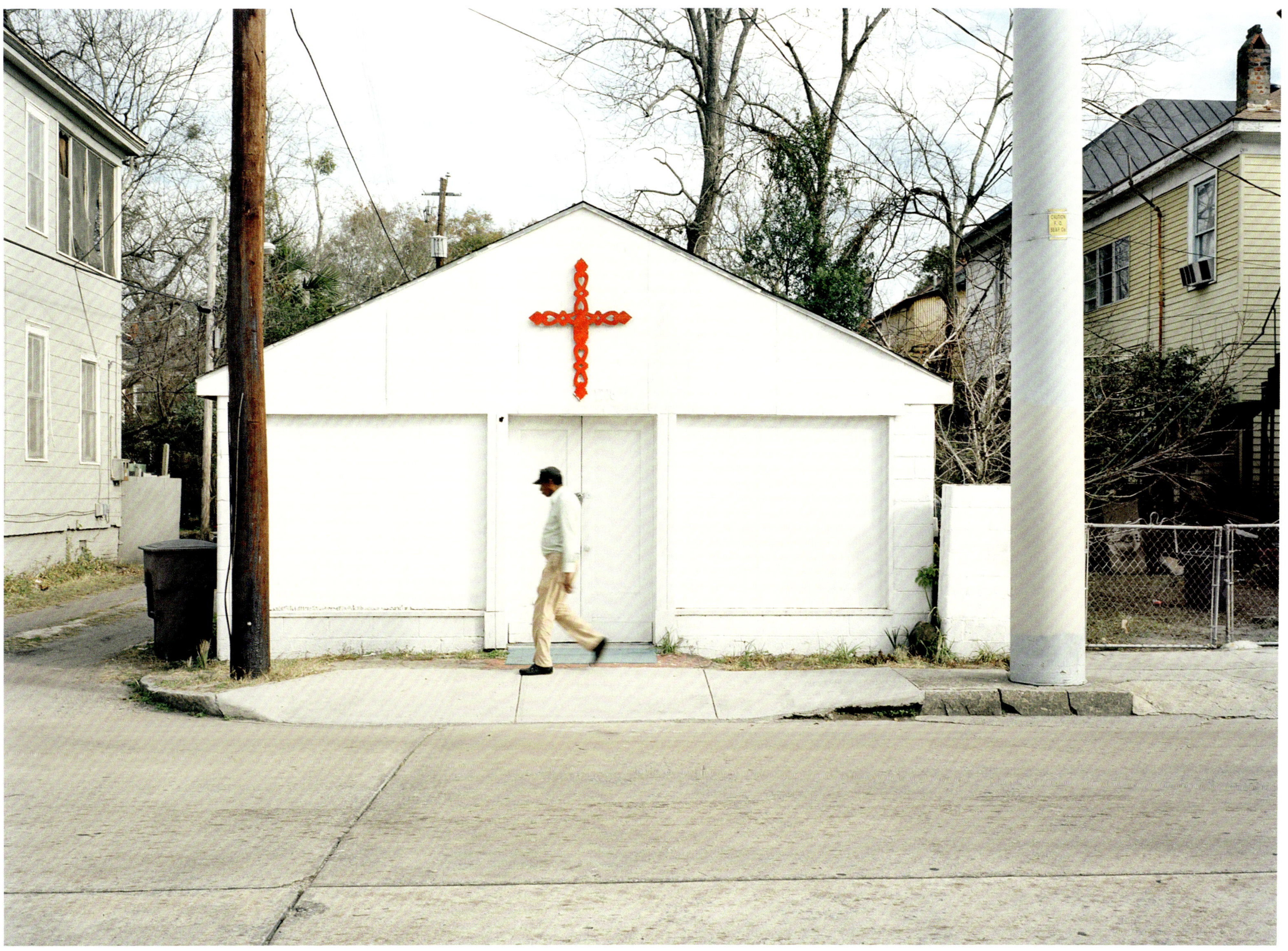

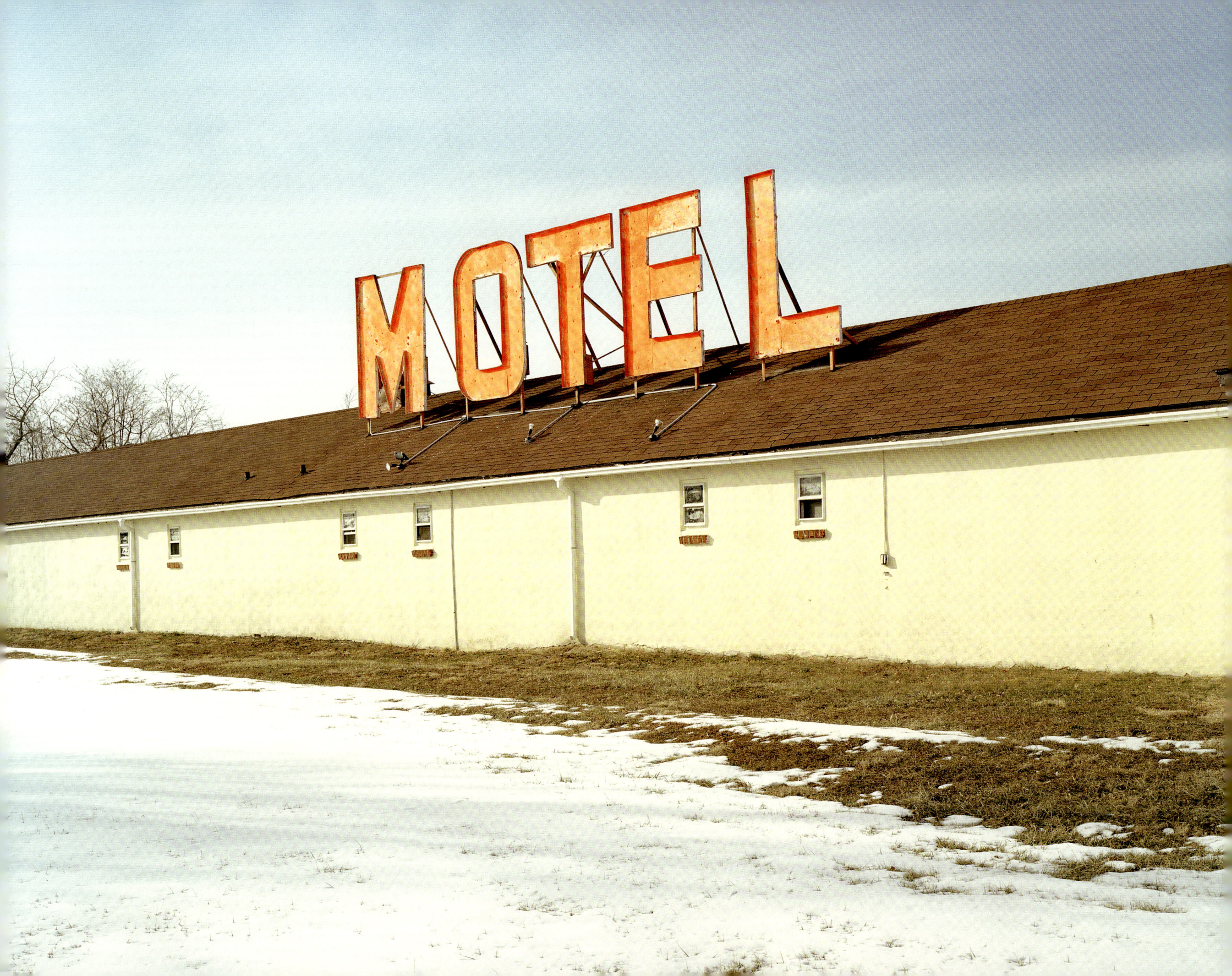
MOTEL

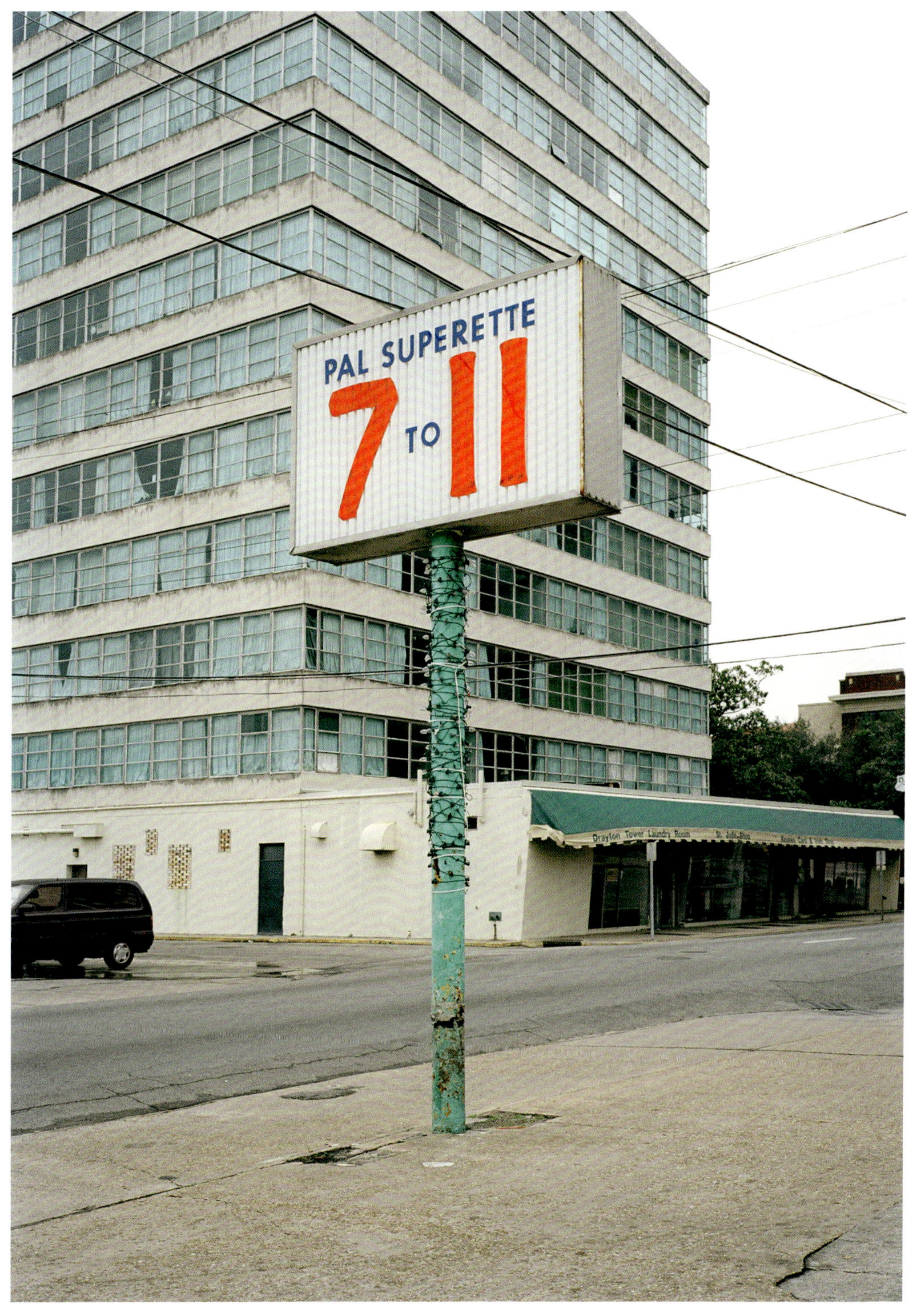

PAL SUPERETTE
7 TO 11

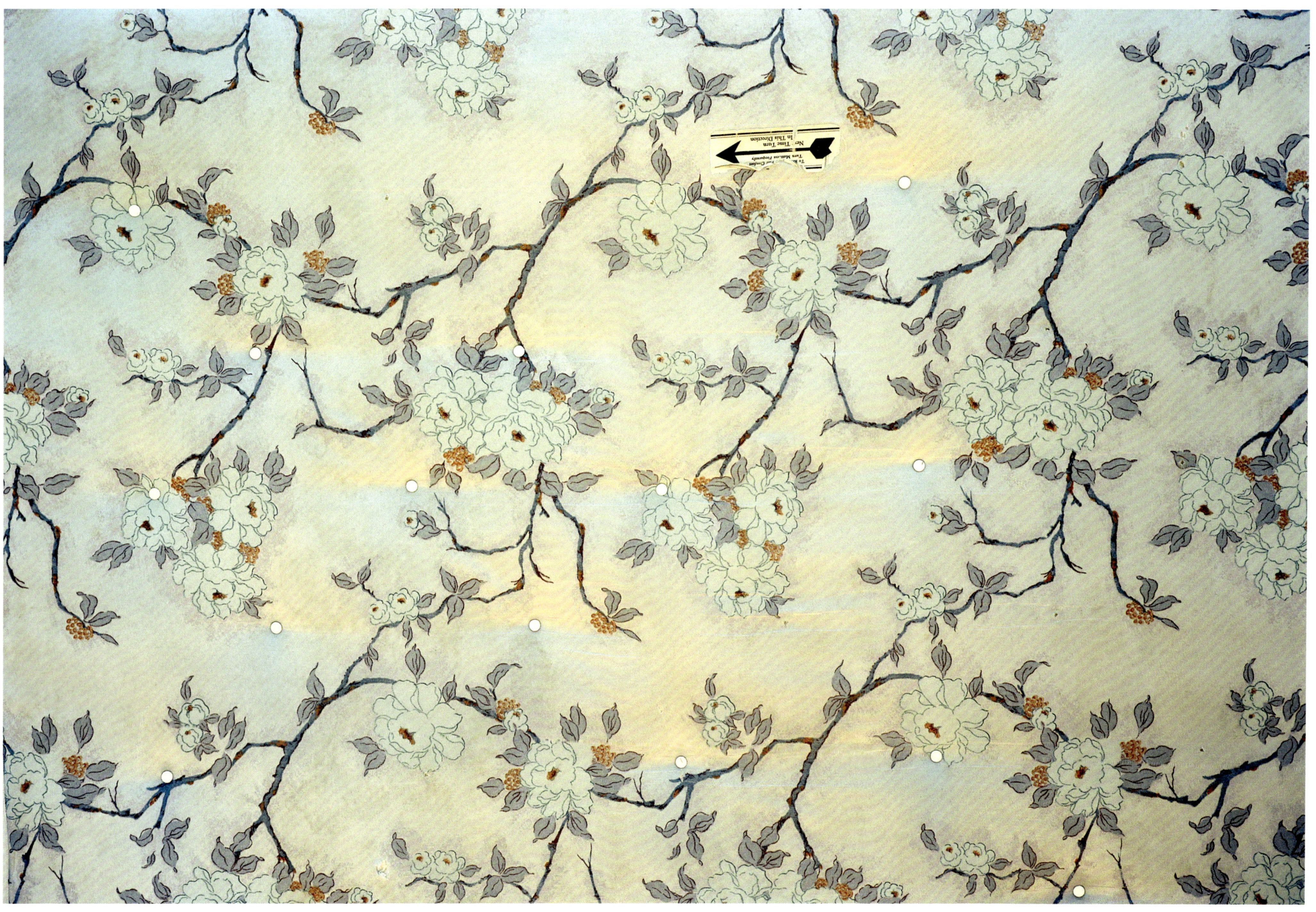

Next Time Turn
In This Direction
To Reduce Seat Comfort
Turn Mat as Frequently

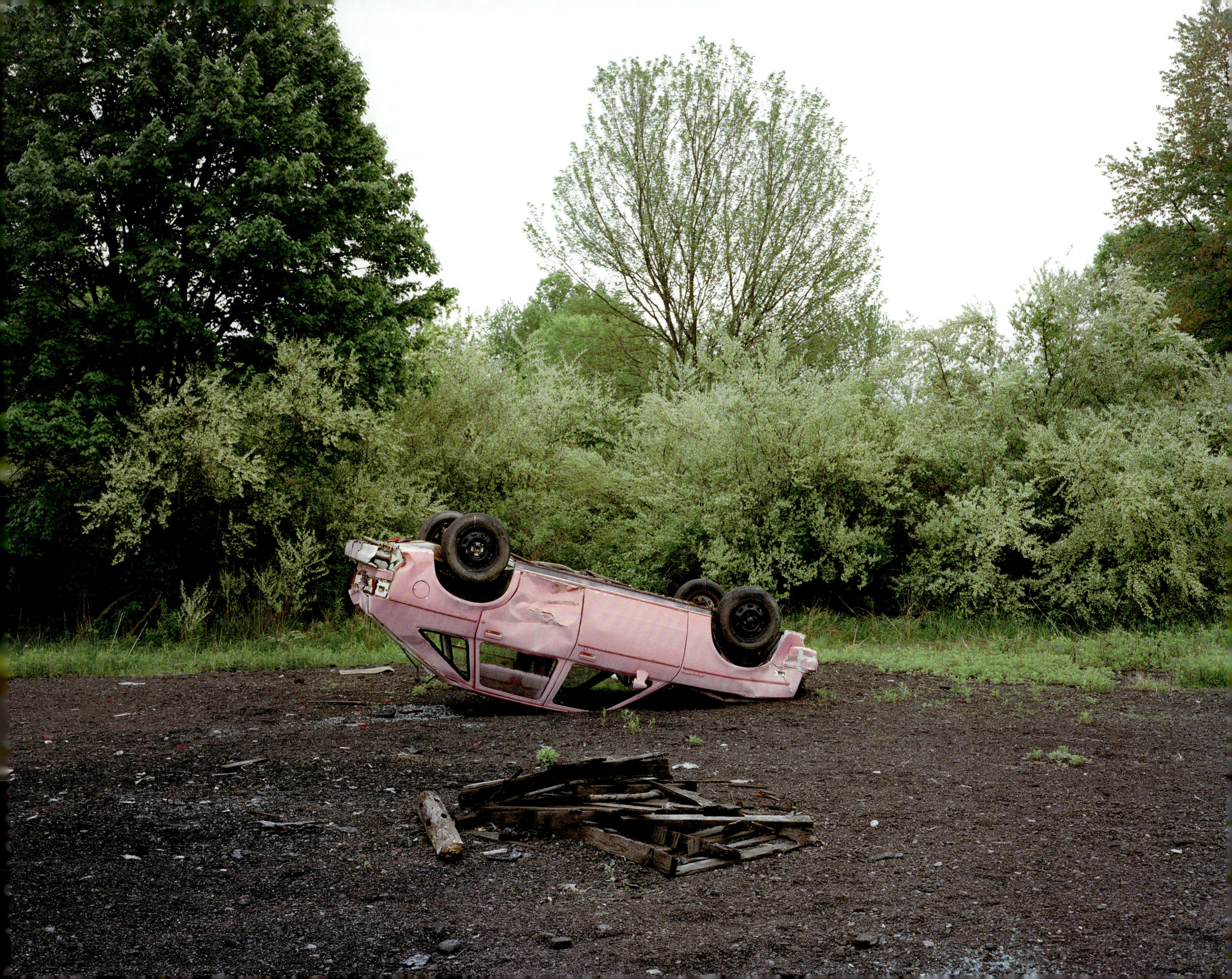

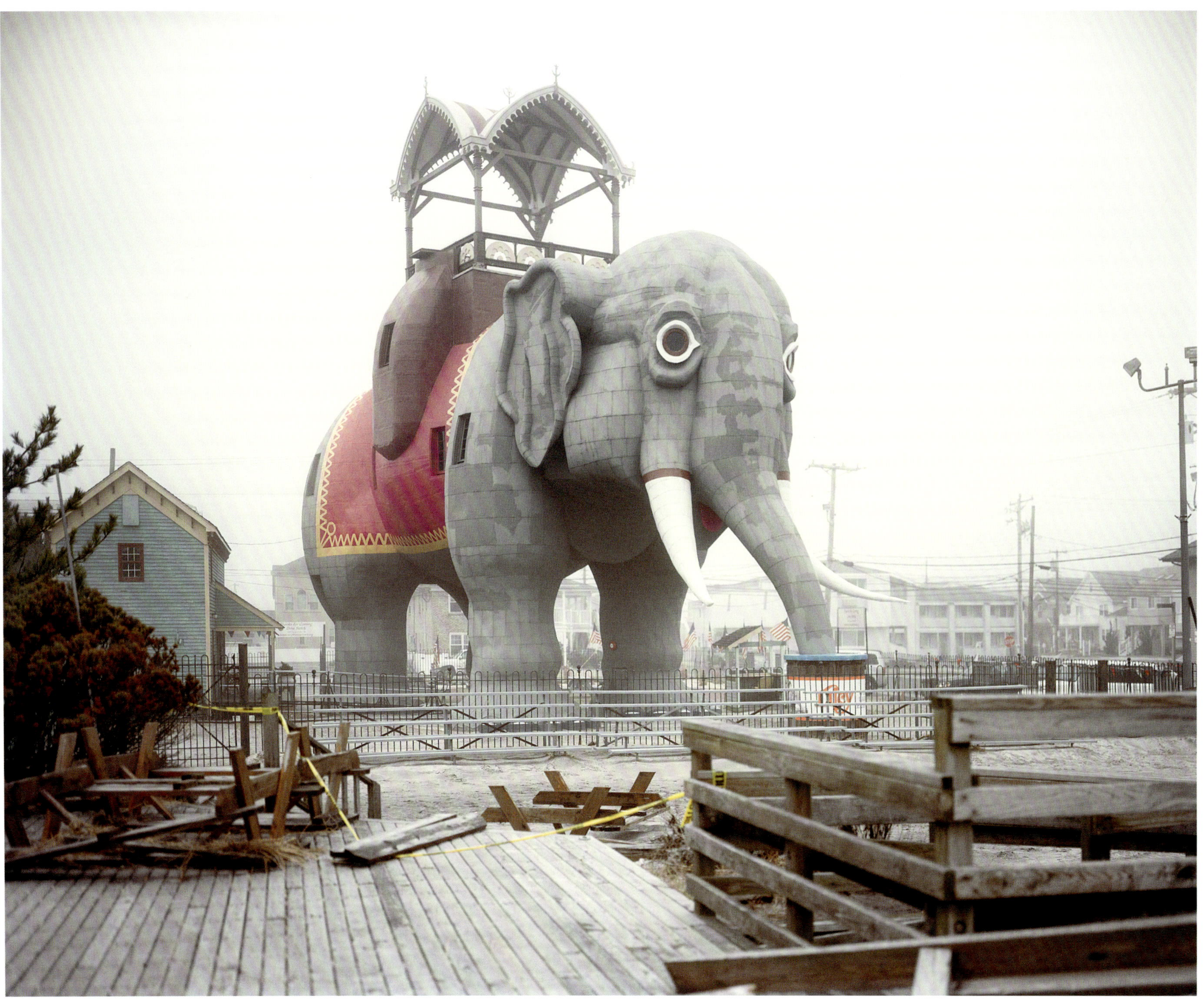

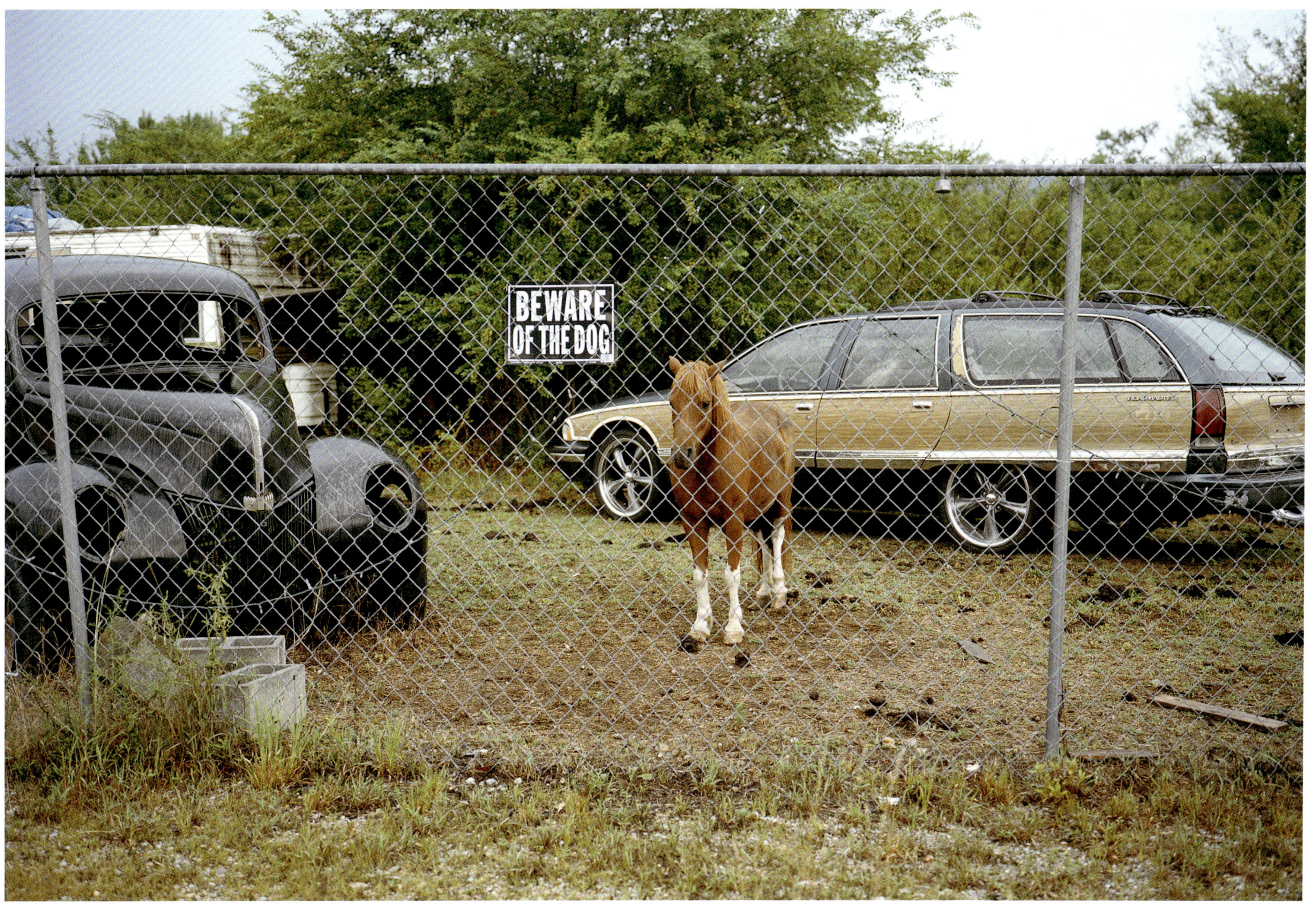

BEWARE
OF THE DOG

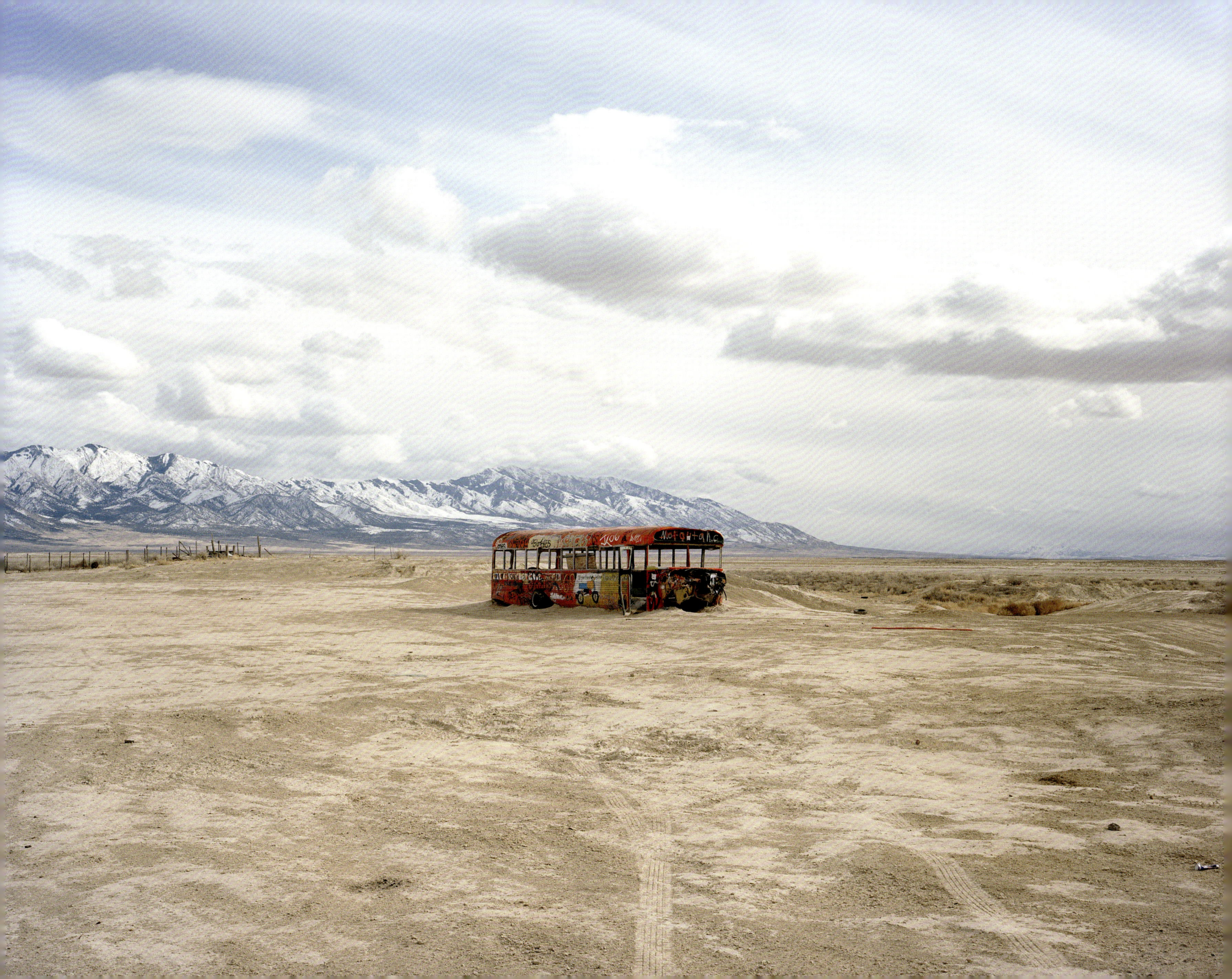

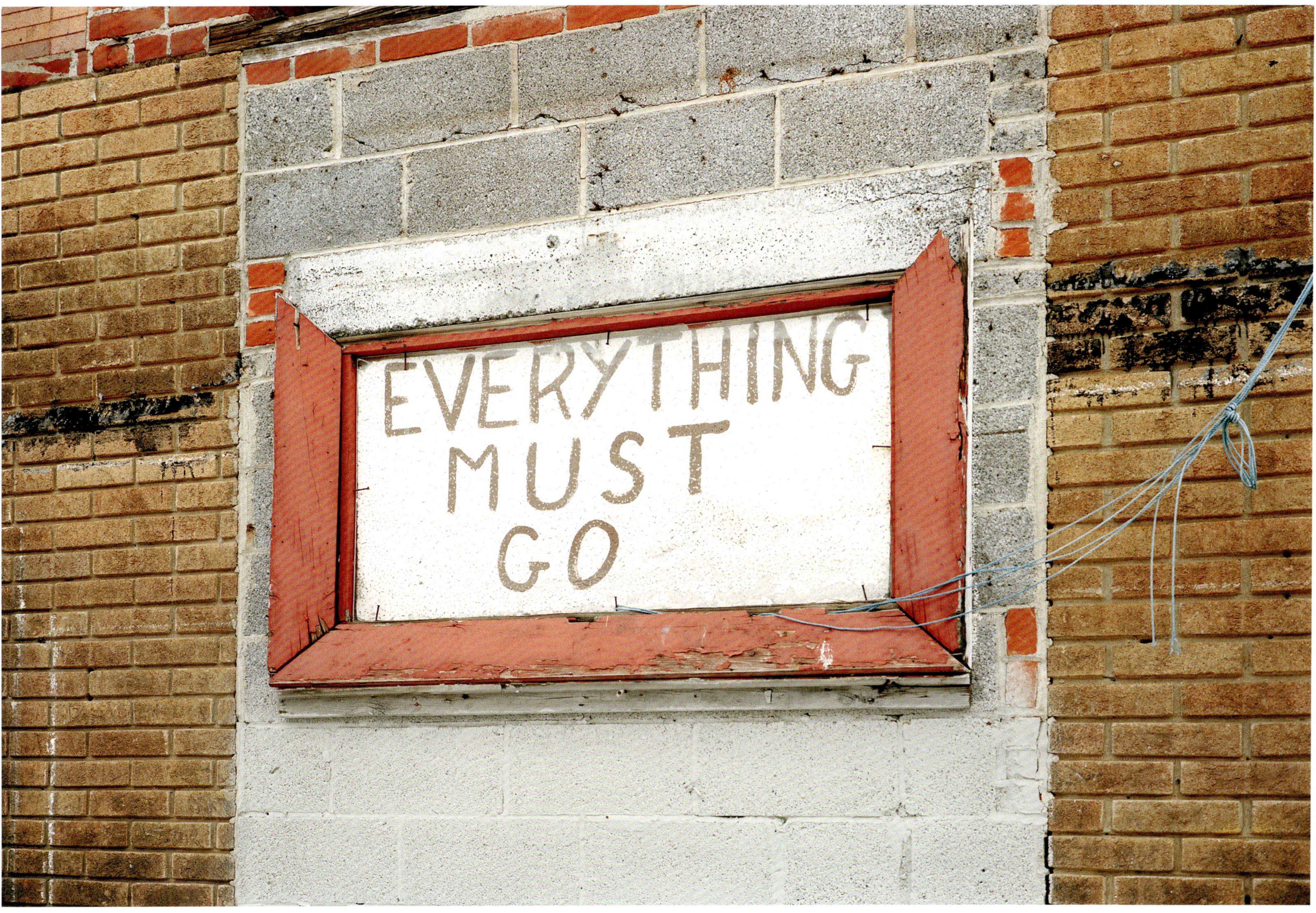

EVERYTHING
MUST
GO

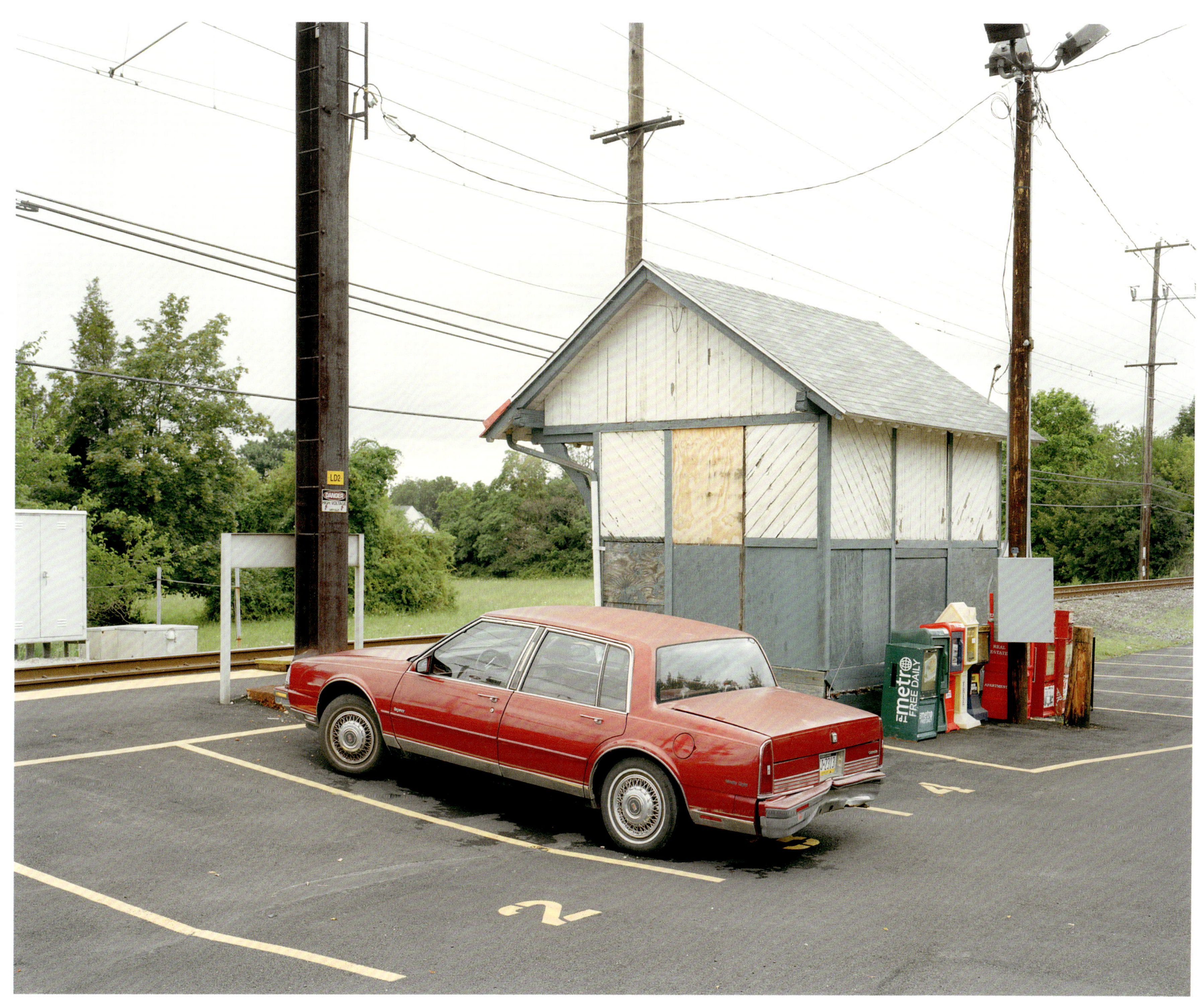

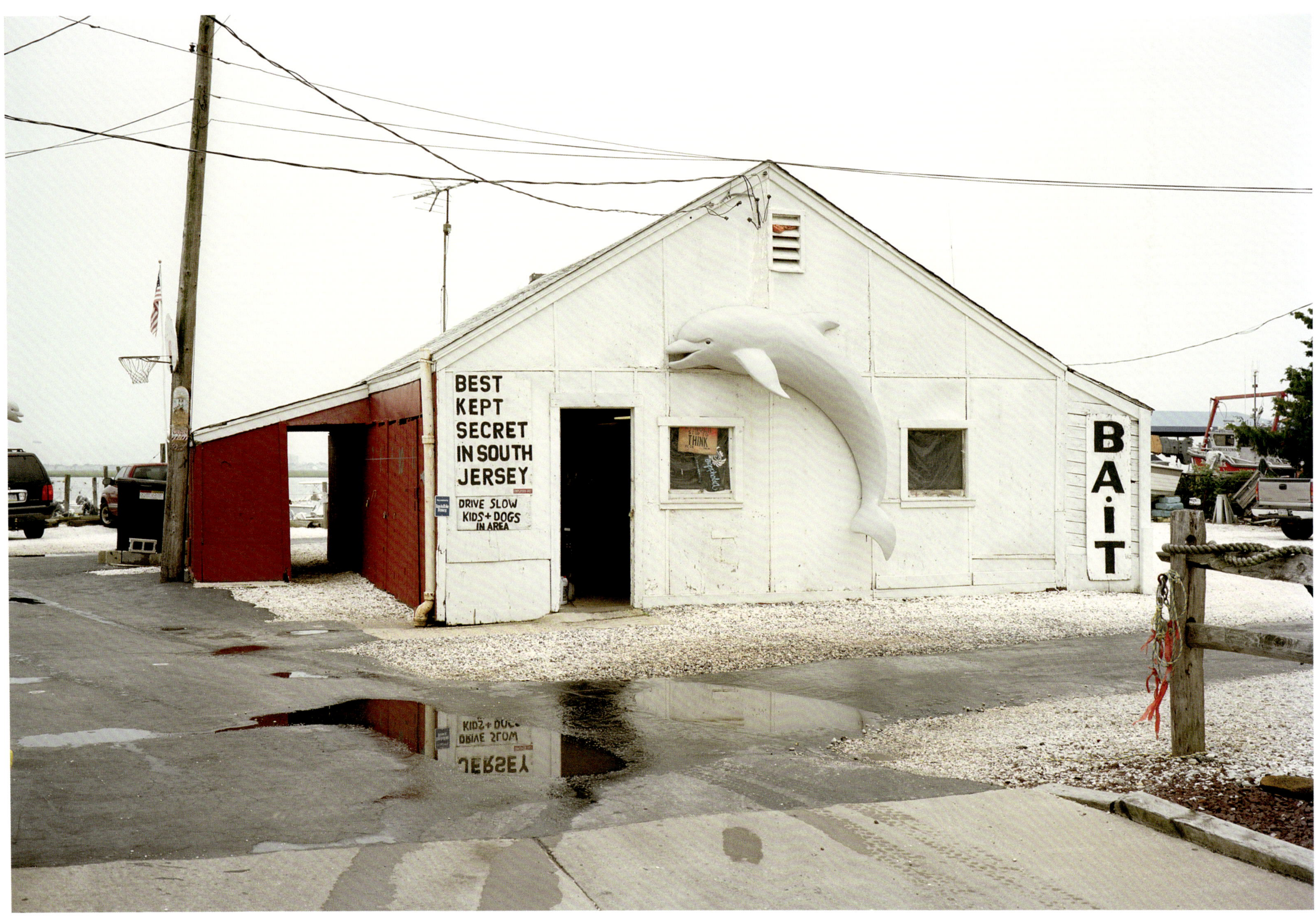
BEST
KEPT
SECRET
IN SOUTH
JERSEY
DRIVE SLOW
KIDS + DOGS
IN AREA
THINK
BAiT

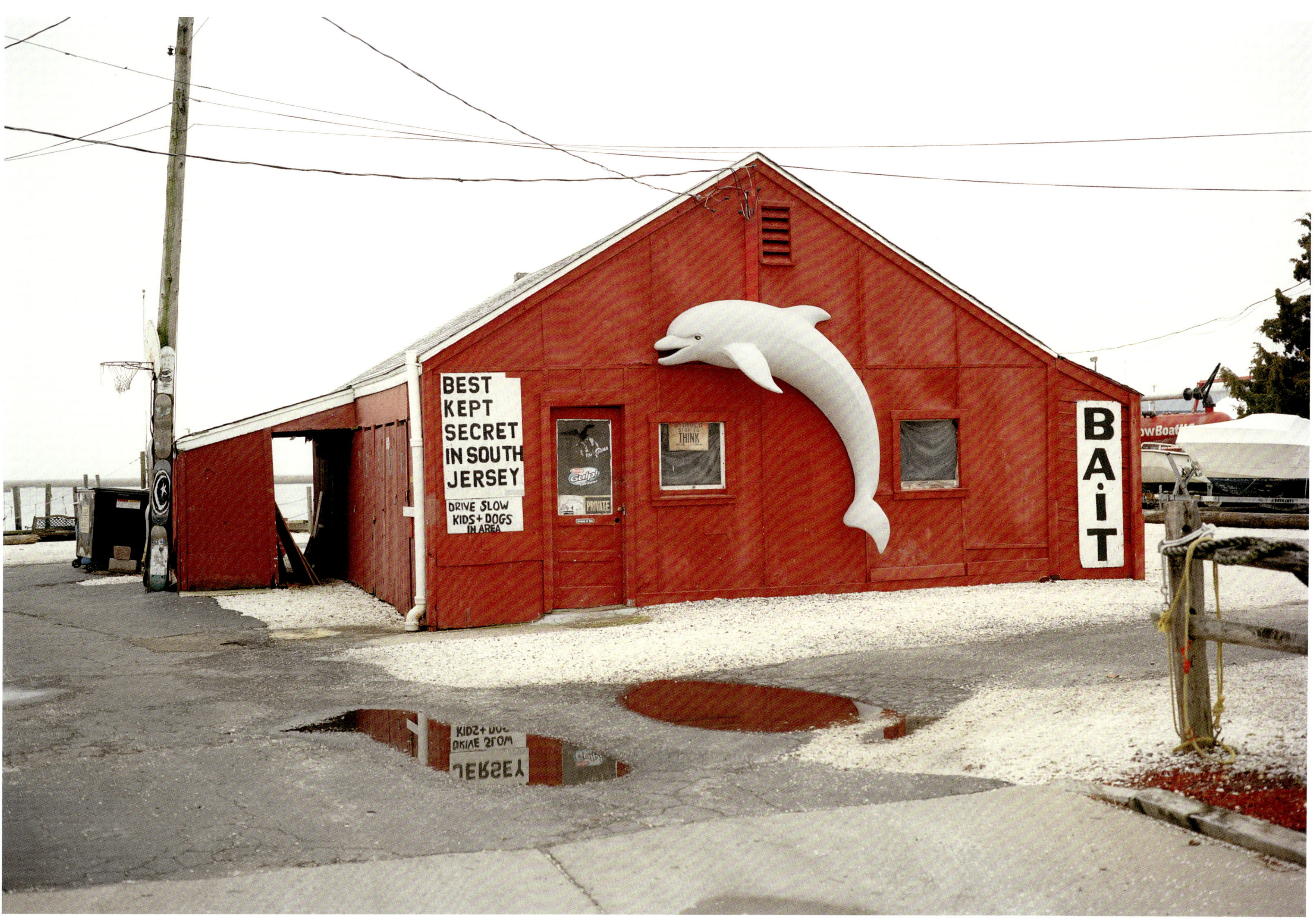
BEST
KEPT
SECRET
IN SOUTH
JERSEY
DRIVE SLOW
KIDS + DOGS
IN AREA
PRIVATE
Gulp!
THINK
BAiT

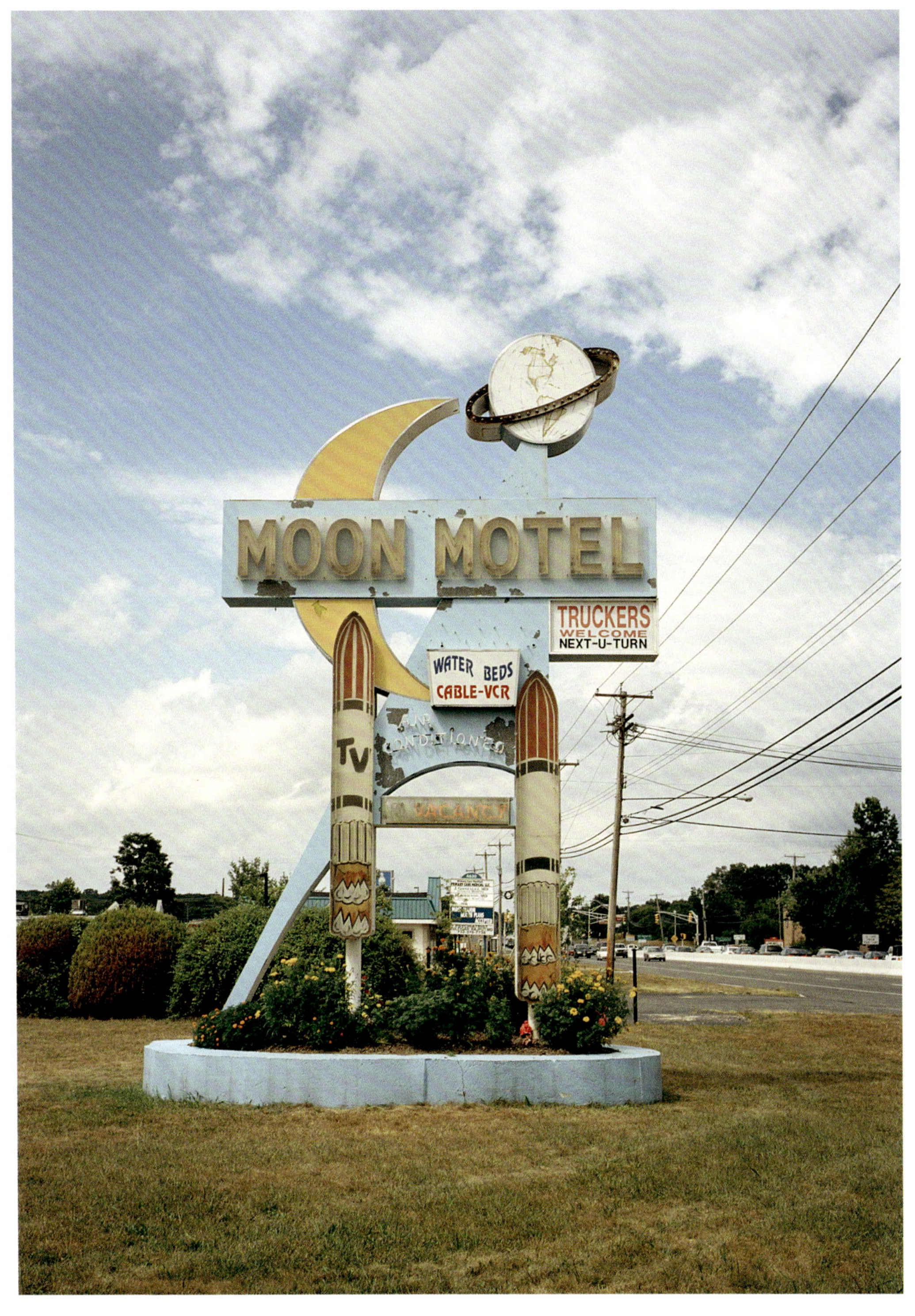

MOON MOTEL
TRUCKERS
WELCOME
NEXT-U-TURN
WATER BEDS
CABLE-VCR
TV
AIR CONDITIONED
VACANCY

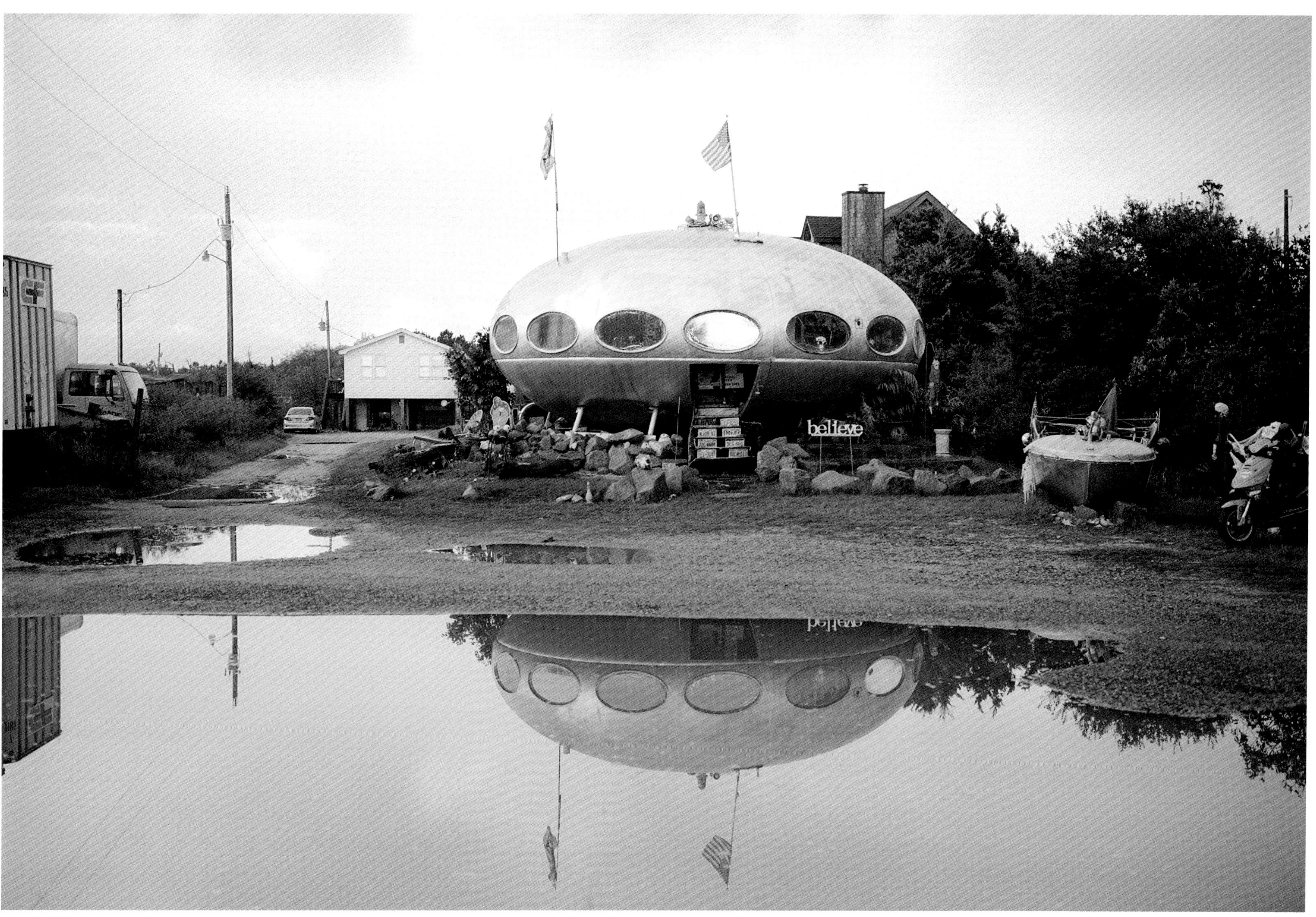

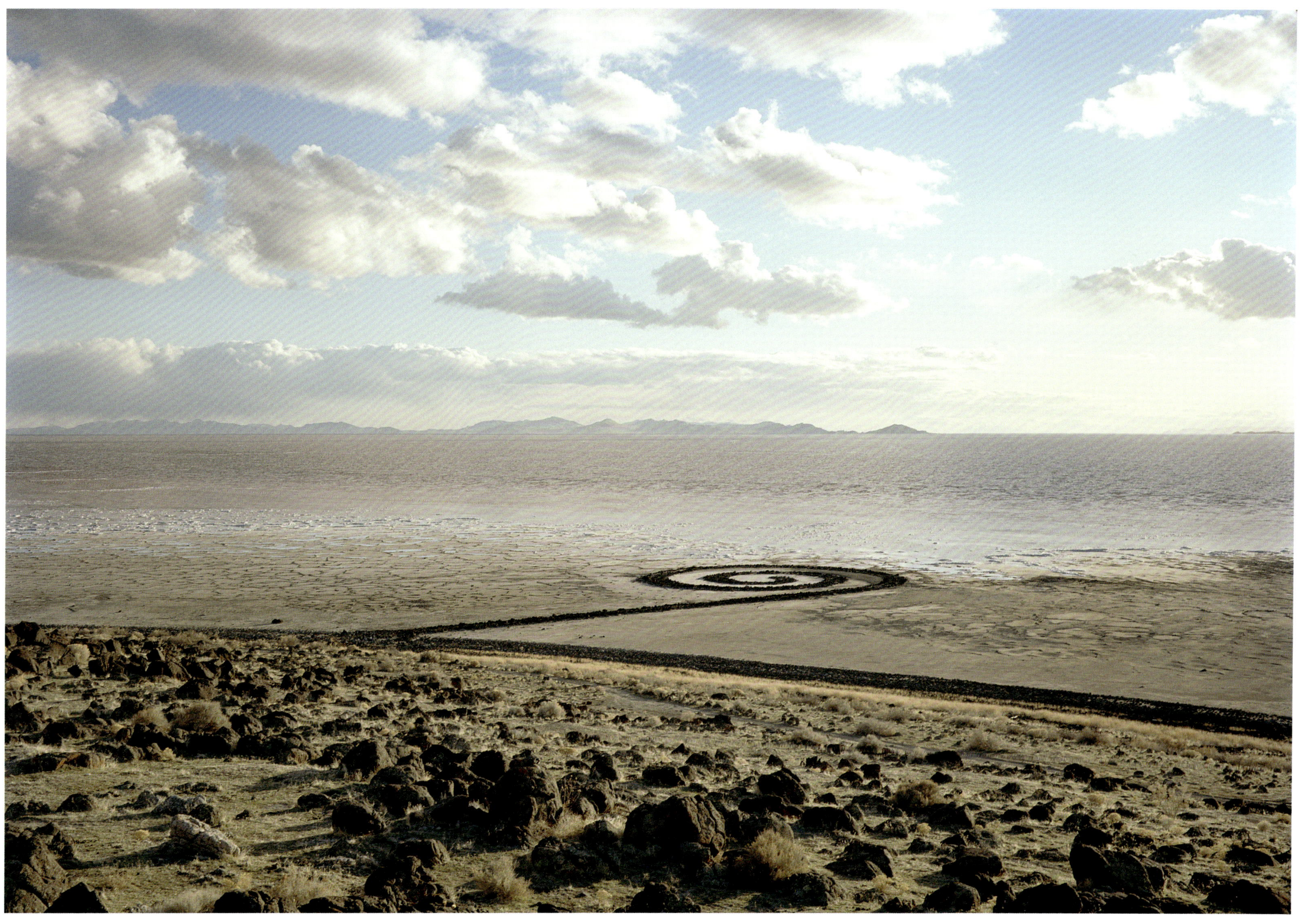

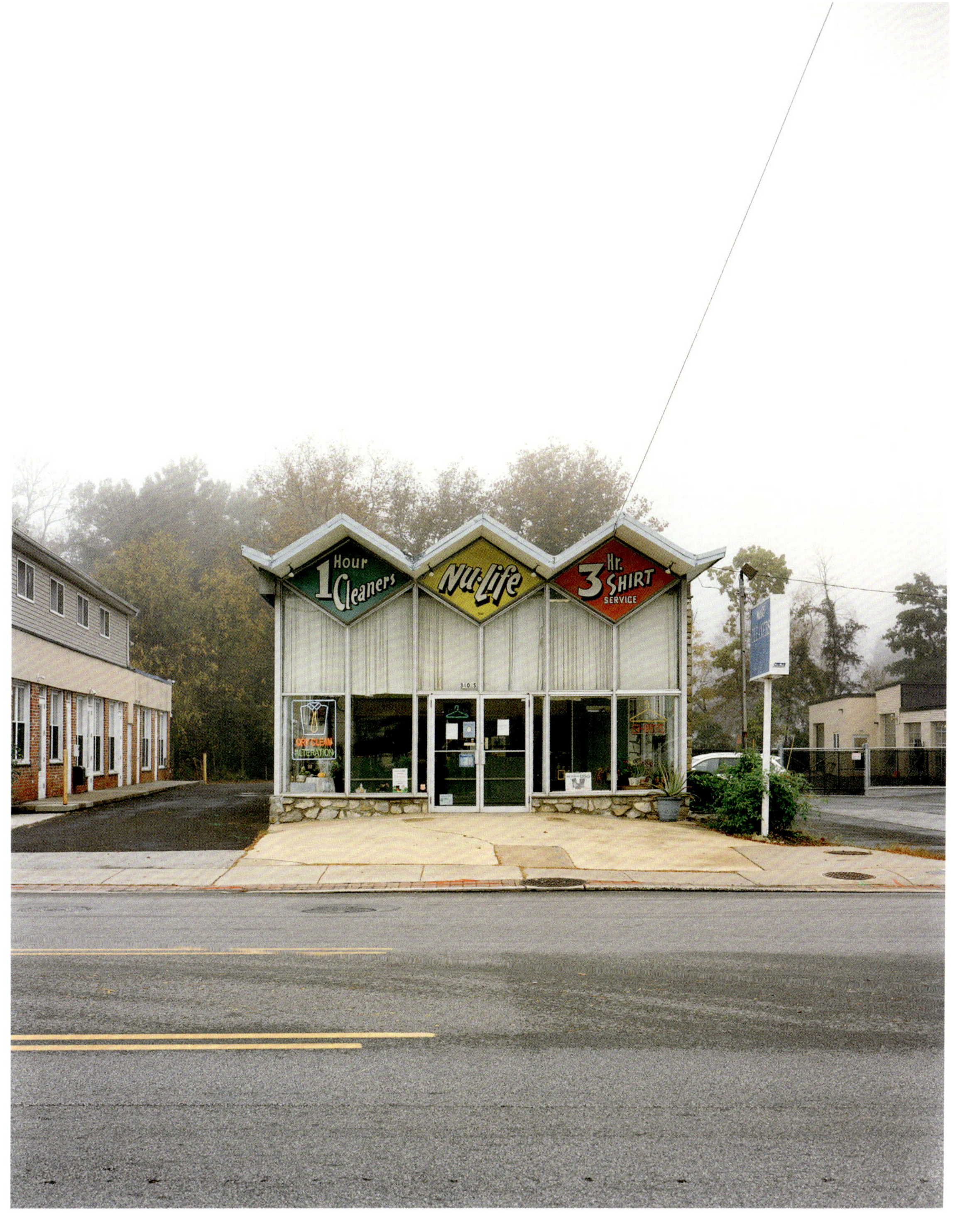

1 Hour Cleaners
Nu-Life
3 Hr. SHIRT SERVICE

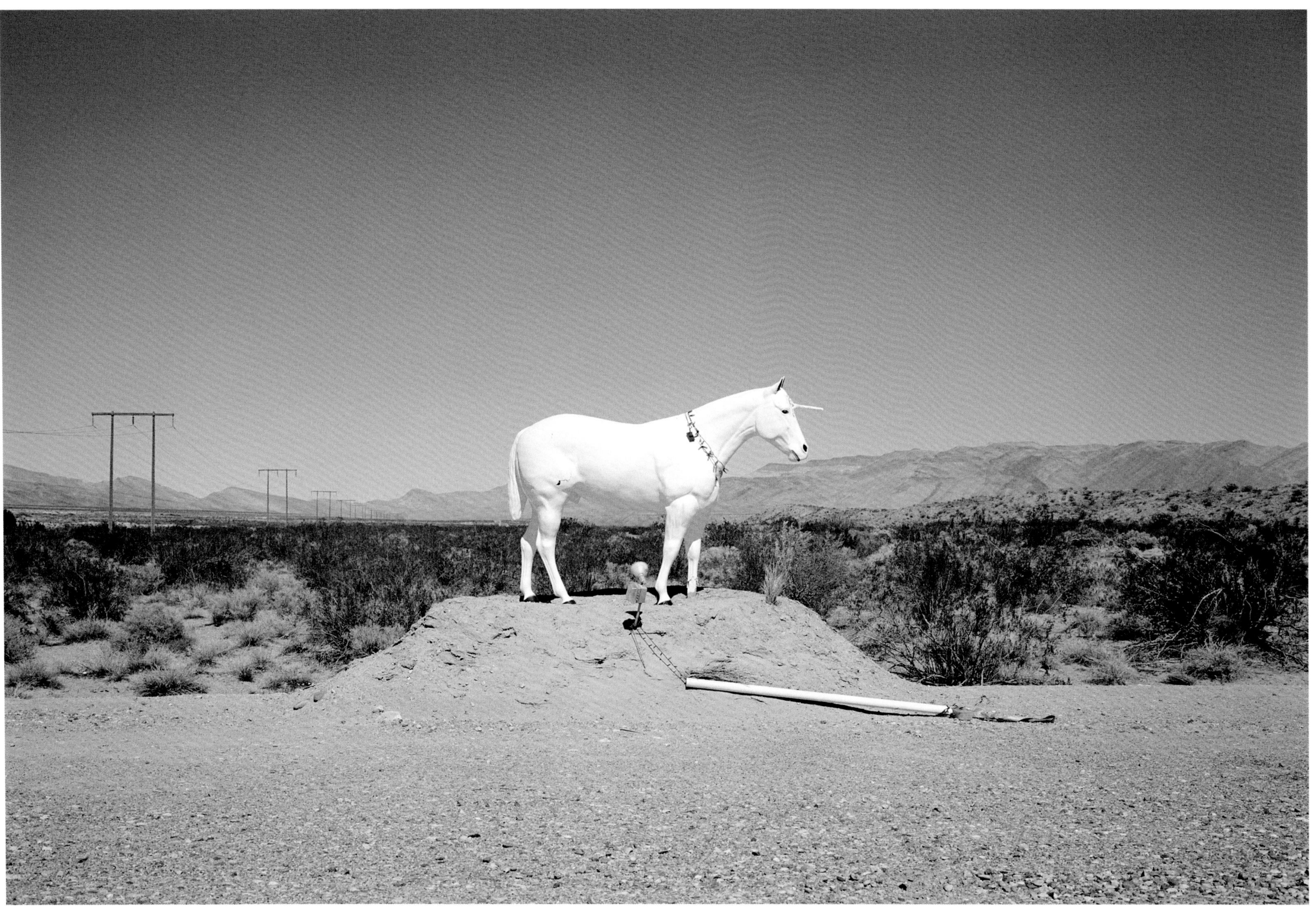

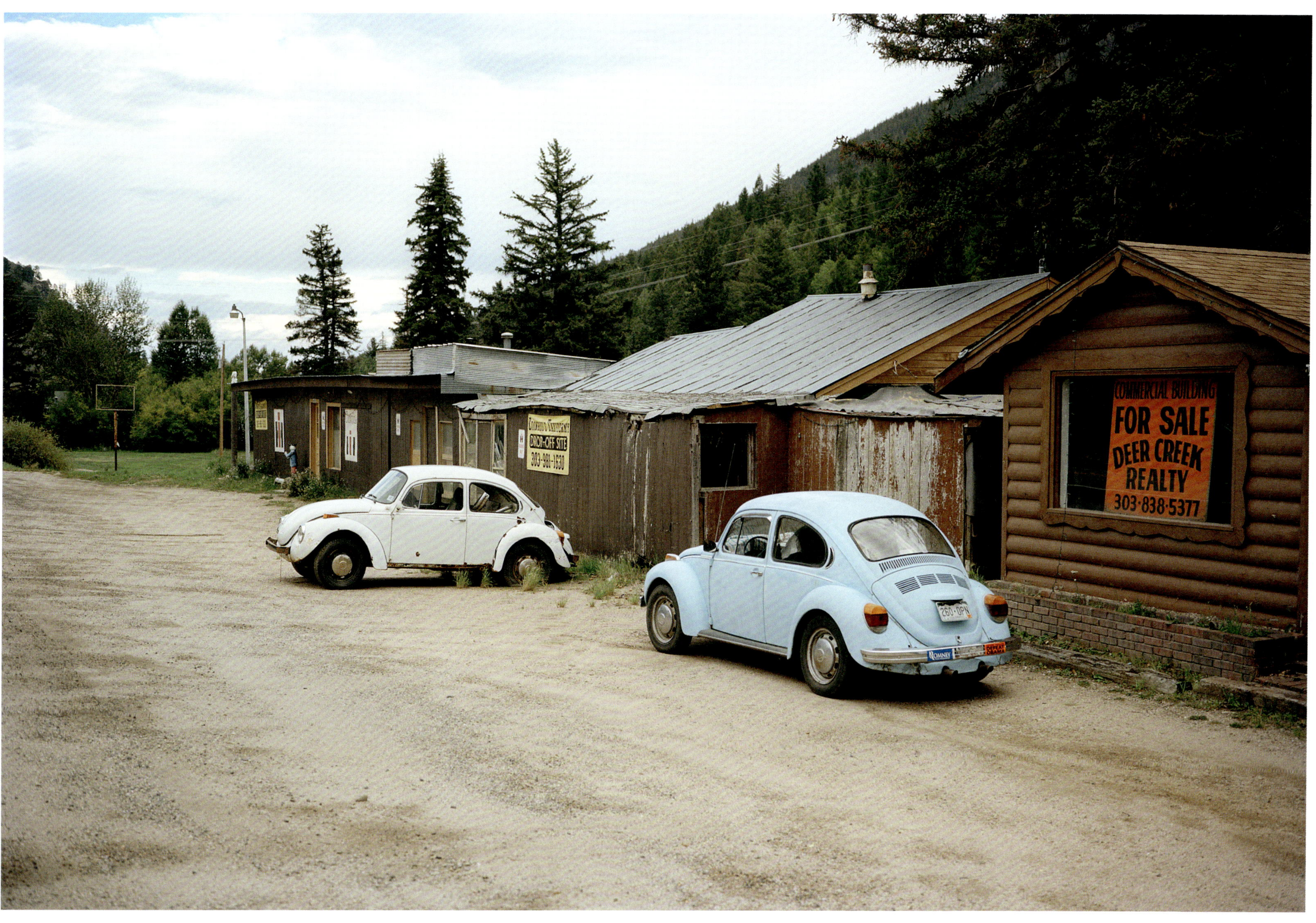
FOR SALE
DEER CREEK
REALTY
303-838-5377

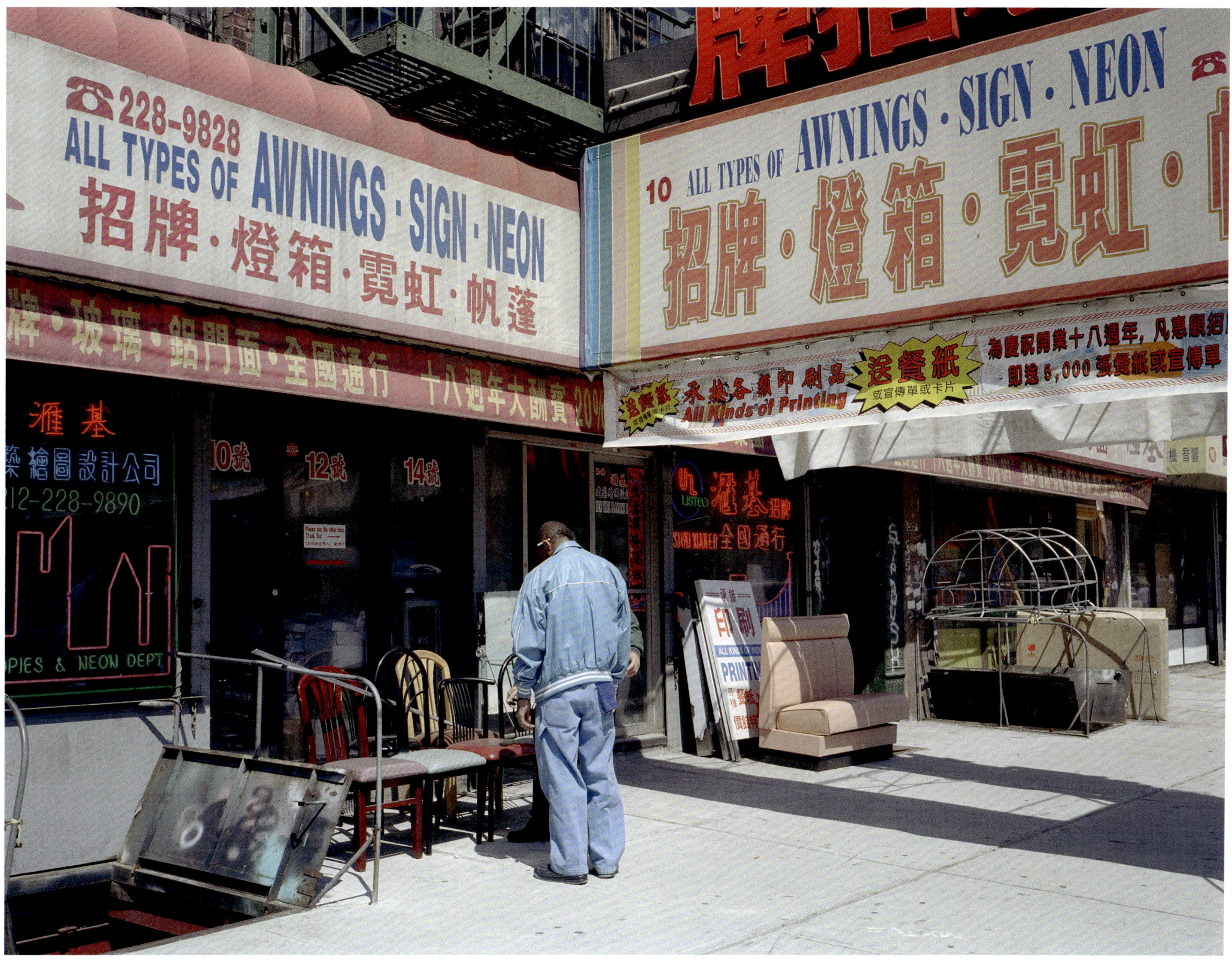

228-9828
ALL TYPES OF AWNINGS · SIGN · NEON
招牌 · 燈箱 · 霓虹 · 帆蓬
牌 · 玻璃 · 鋁門面 · 全國通行 十八週年大酬賓 20%
滙基
建築繪圖設計公司
212-228-9890
PIES & NEON DEPT.
10號 12號 14號
10 ALL TYPES OF AWNINGS · SIGN · NEON
招牌 · 燈箱 · 霓虹 · 中
承接各類印刷品 送餐紙 為慶祝開業十八週年, 凡惠顧招
All Kinds of Printing 或宣傳單或卡片 即送5,000張餐紙或宣傳單
滙基 招牌
SIGN MAKER 全國通行
印刷
ALL KINDS OF NEON
PRINTI

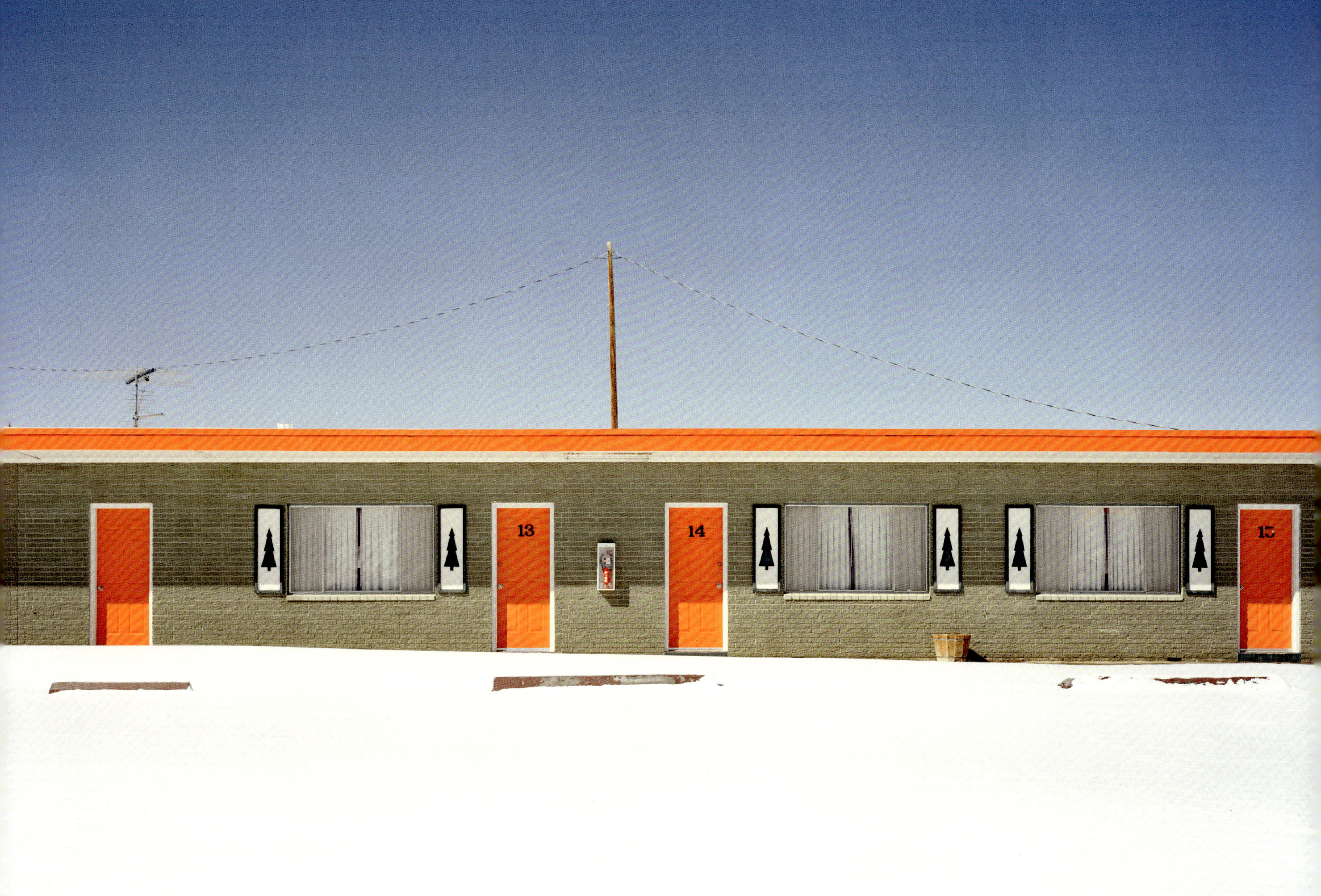

13
14
13

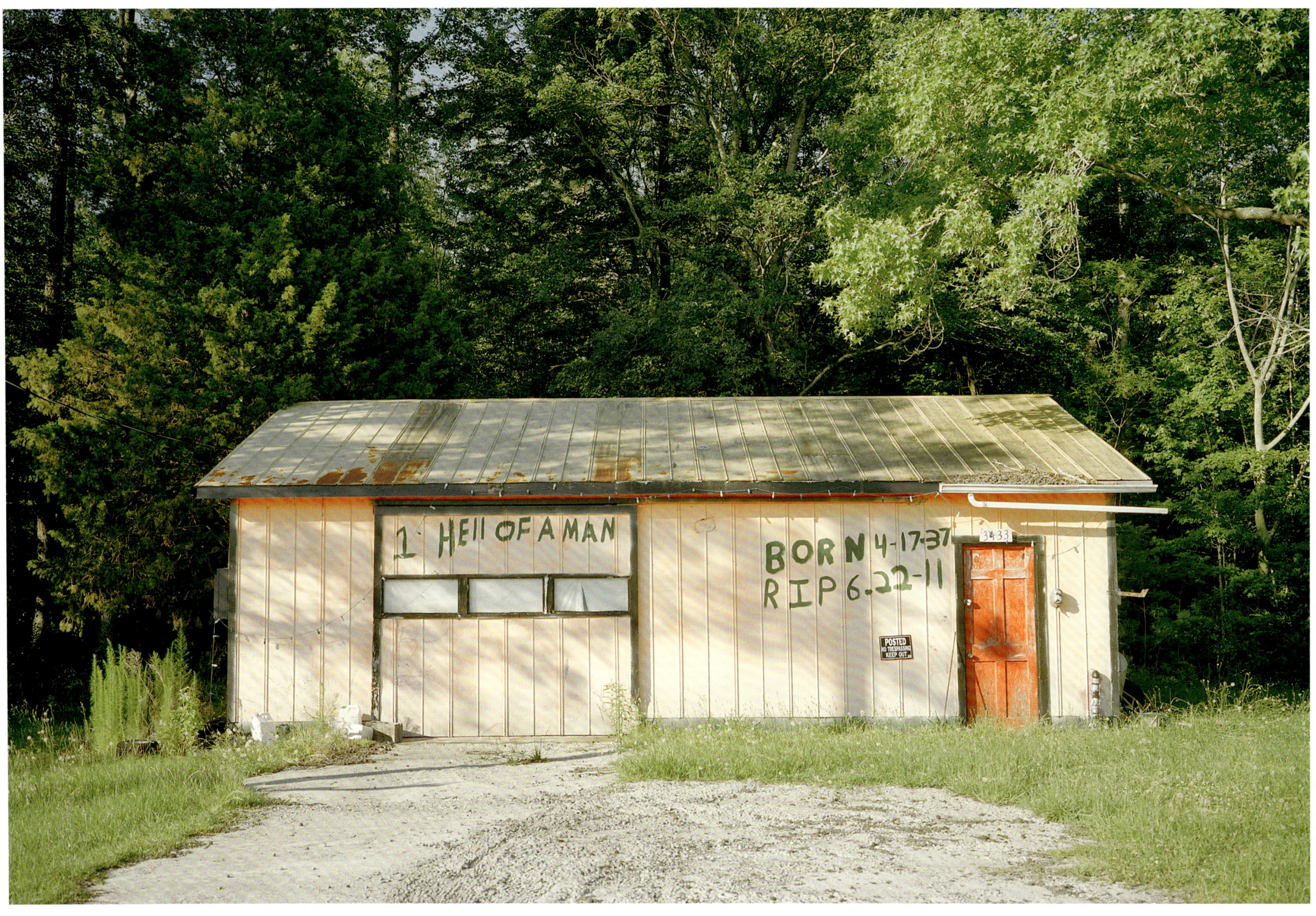
1 HEll OF A MAN
BORN 4-17-37
RIP 6-22-11
3433
POSTED
NO TRESPASSING
KEEP OUT

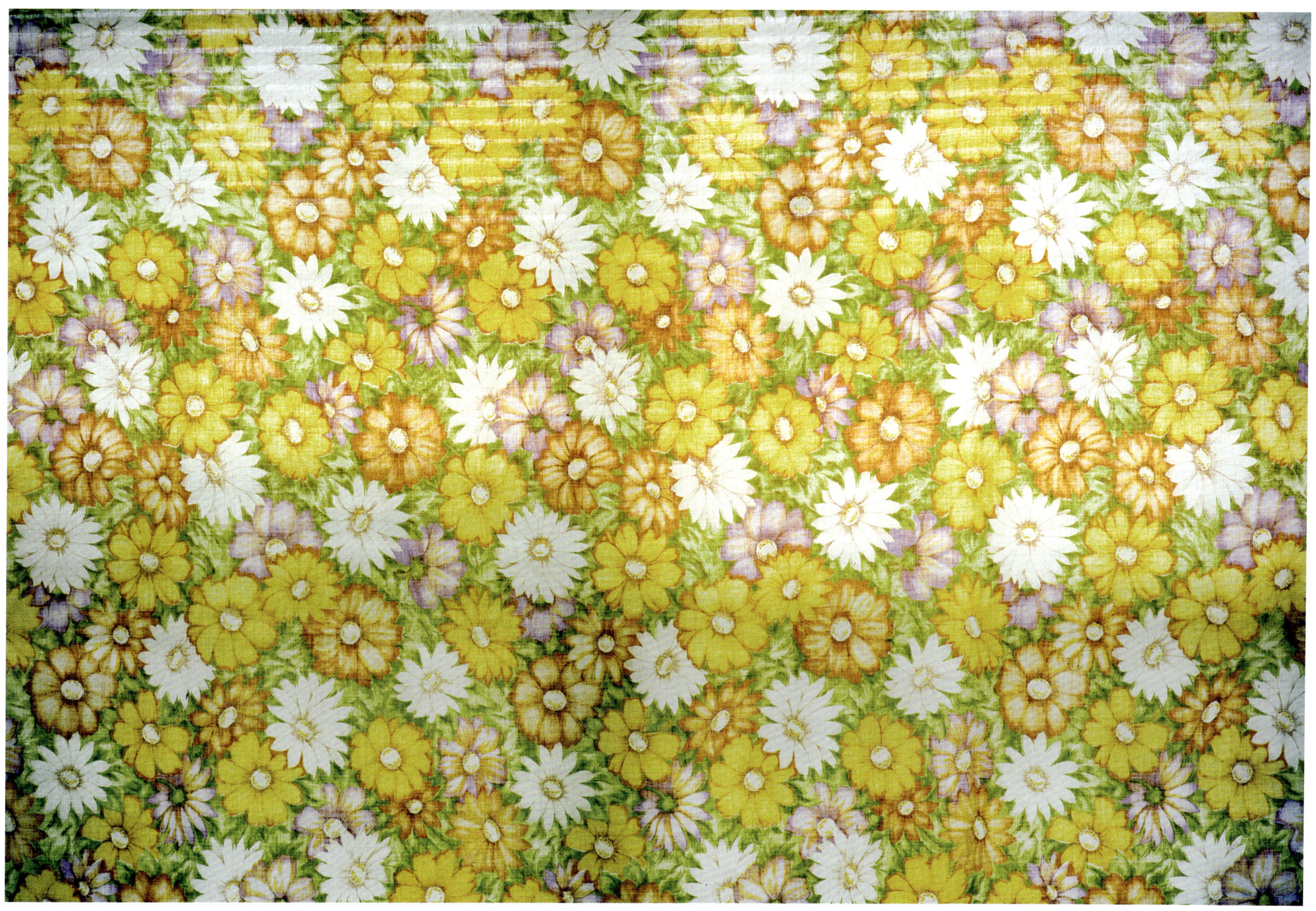

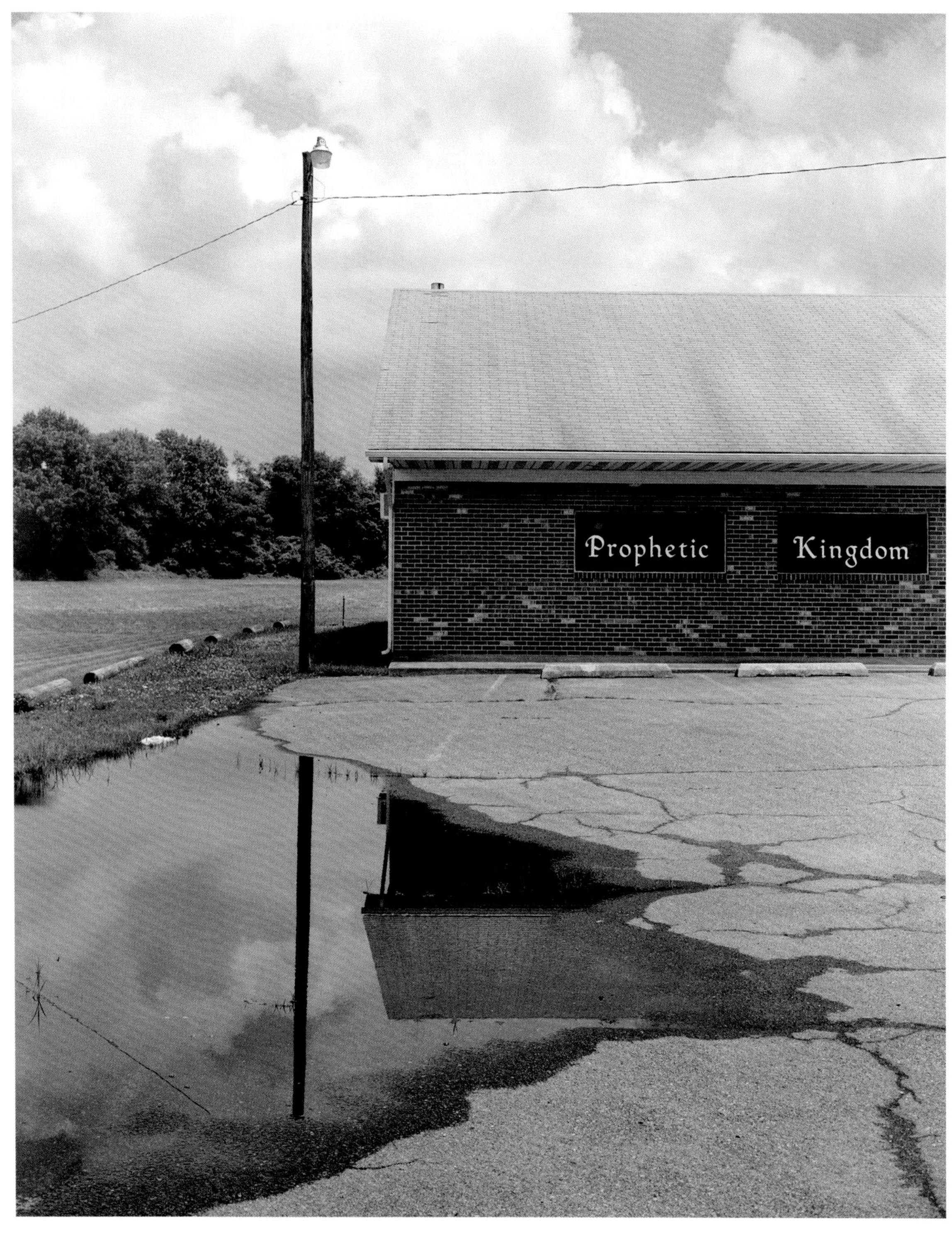
Prophetic   Kingdom

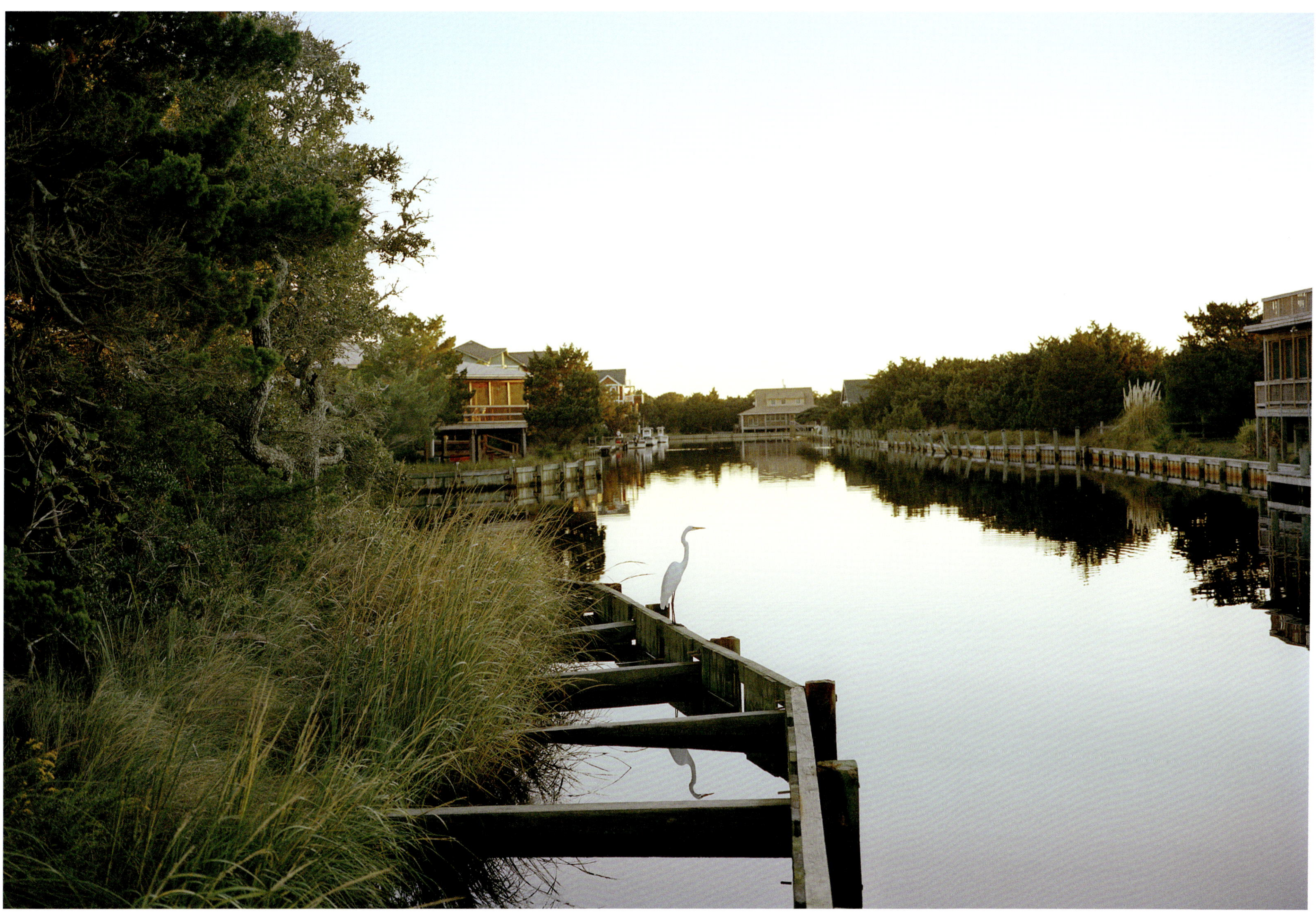

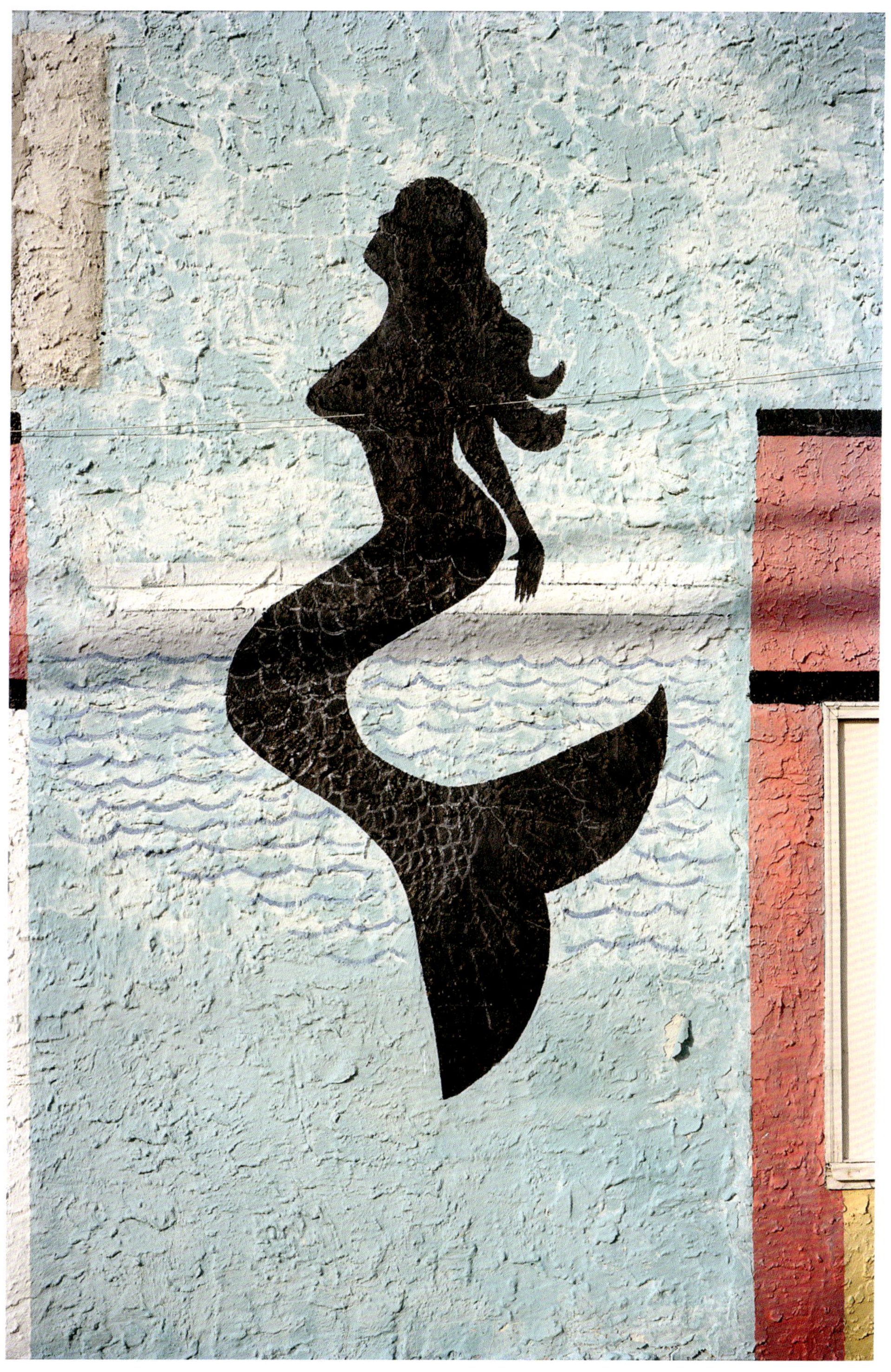

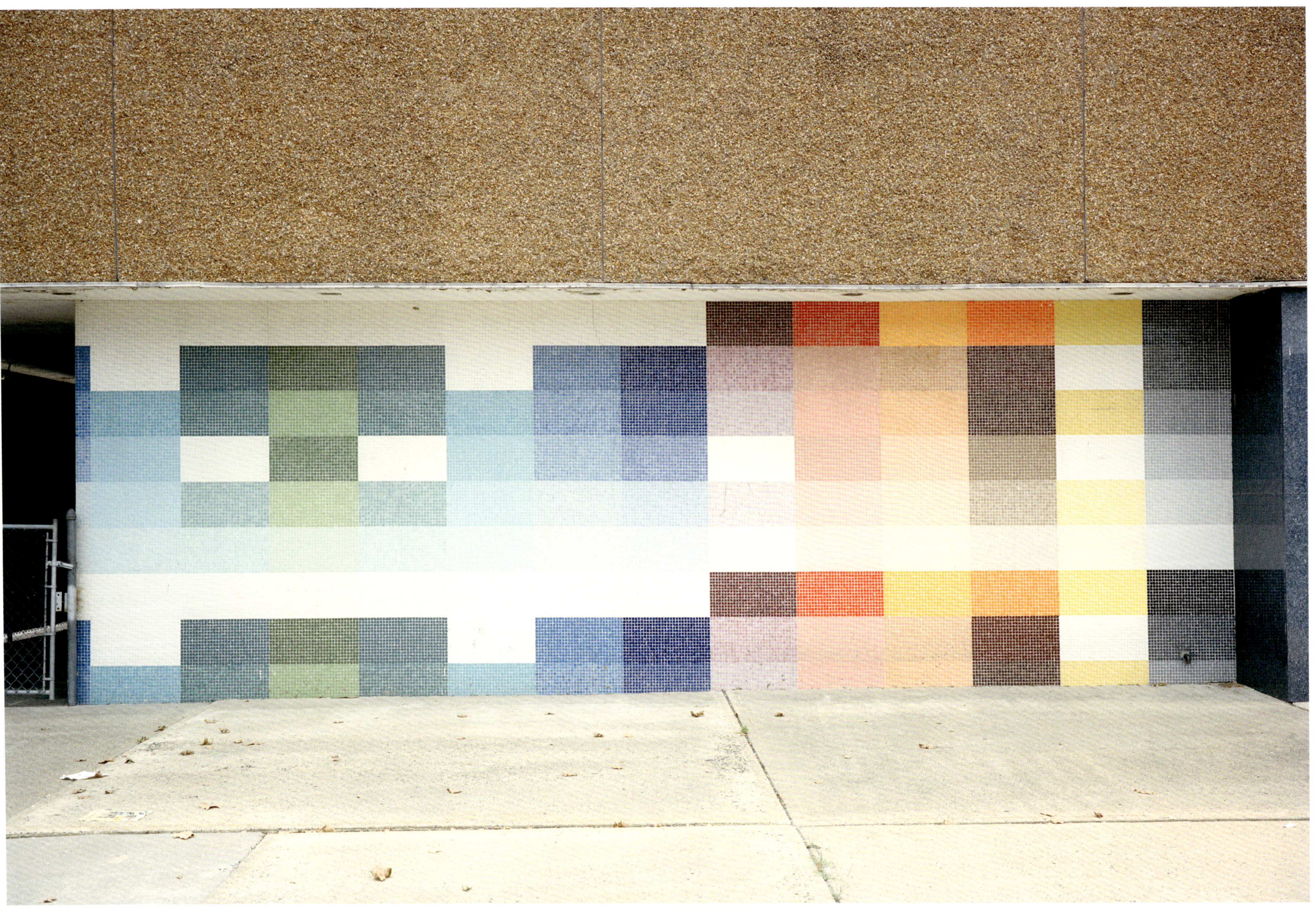

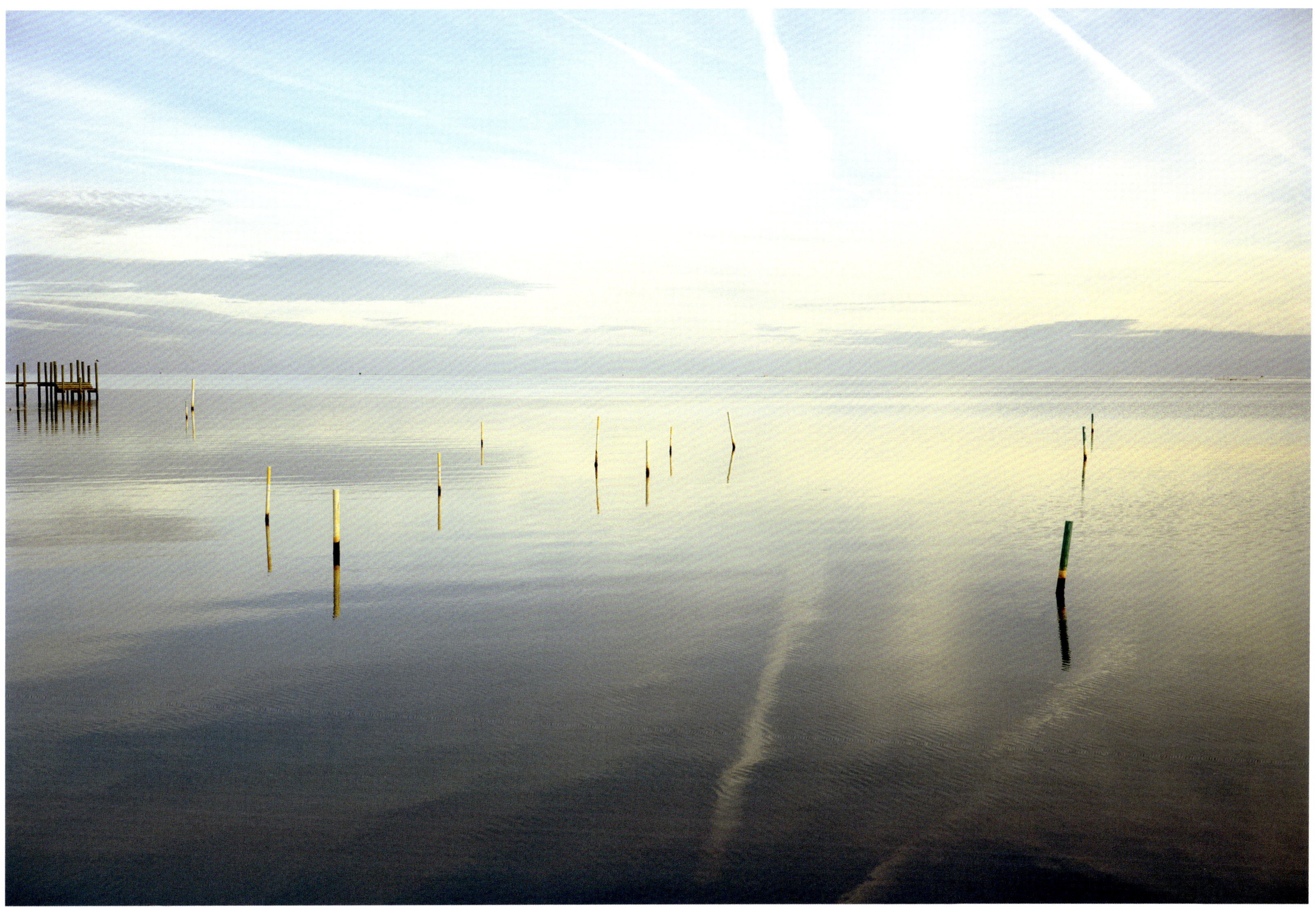

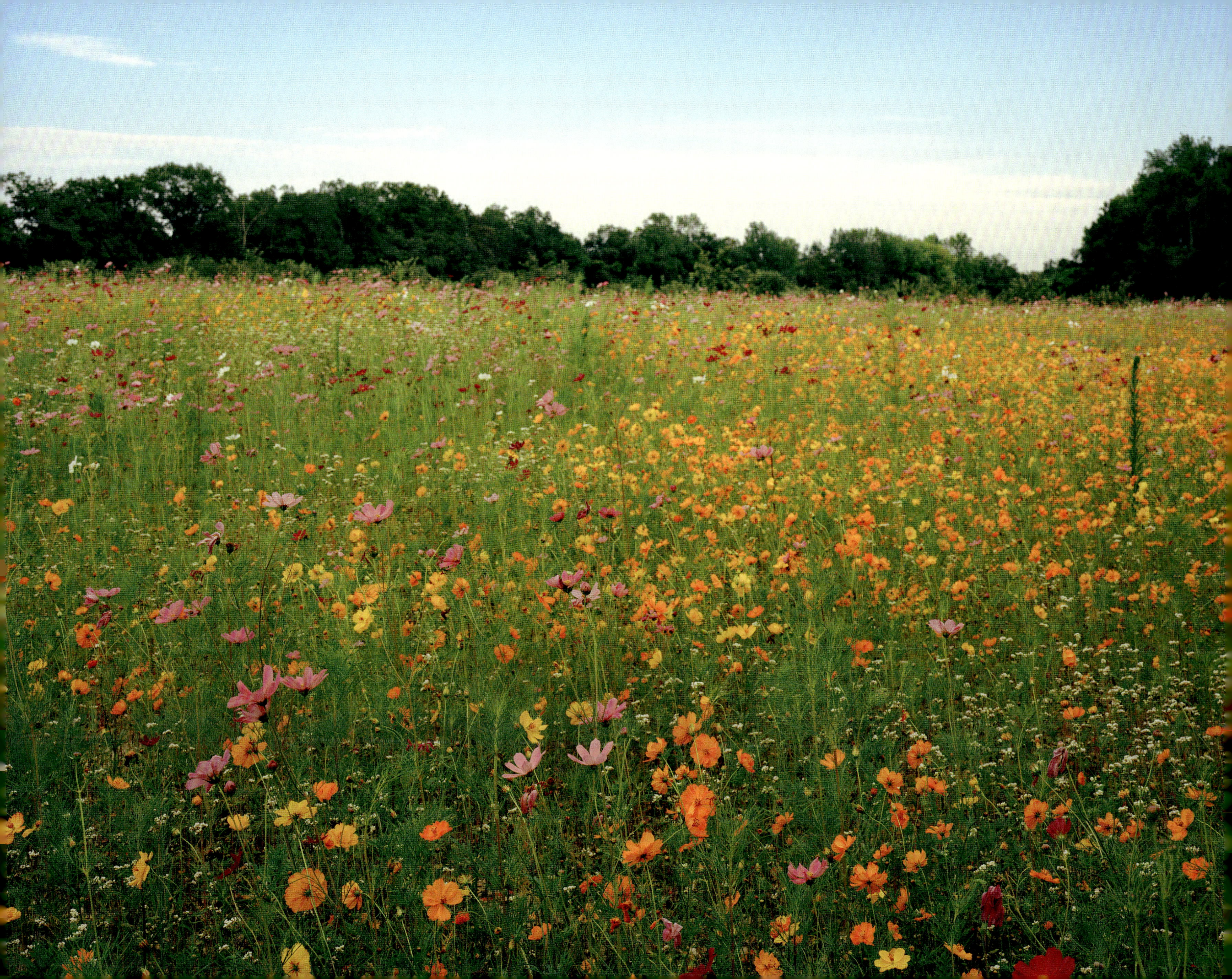

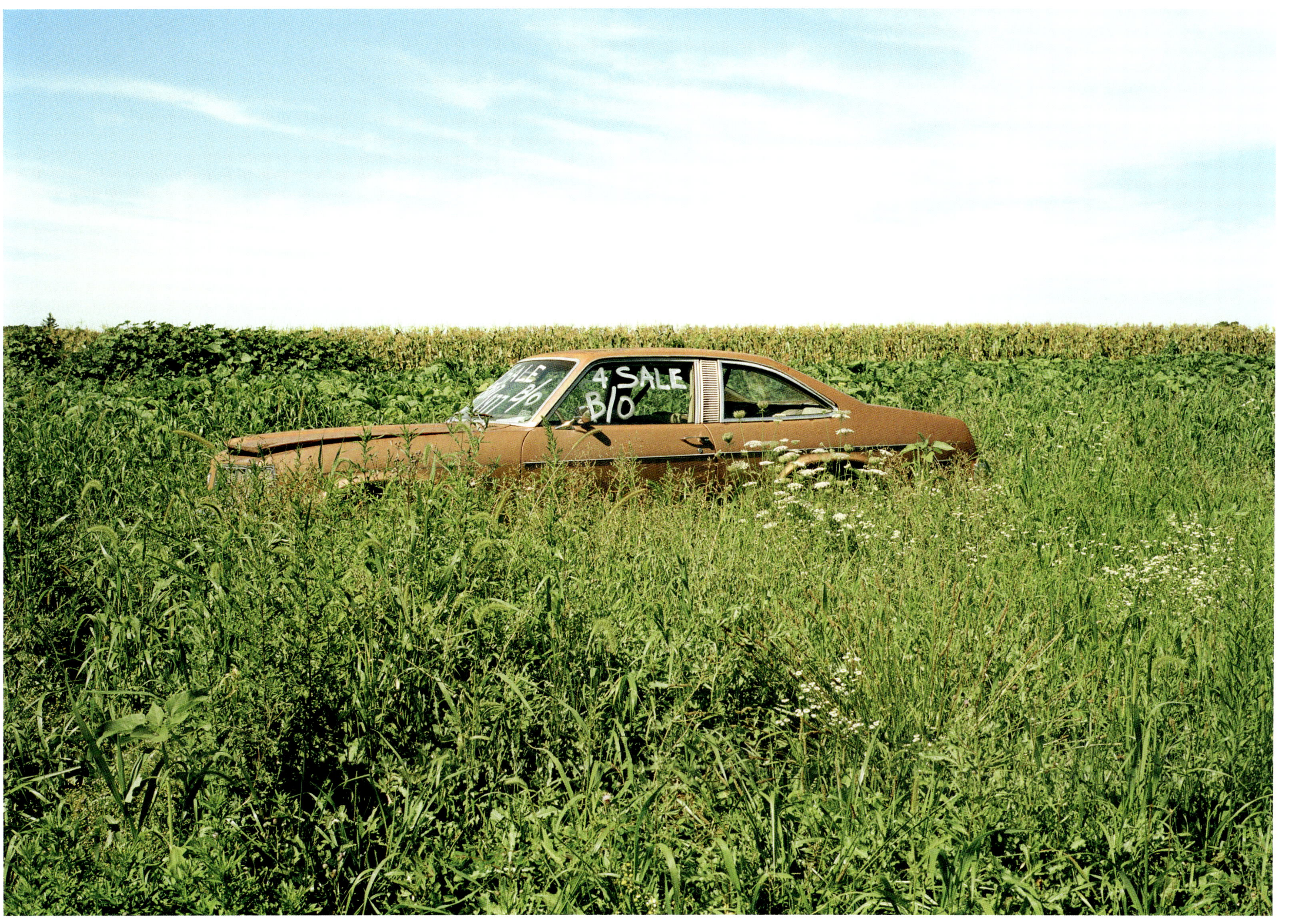
4 SALE
B/O

PLATELIST

PEDESTRIAN SECRETS OF THE UNIVERSE

Prophetic Kingdom is a world of material color, the color of light as the day fades and atmosphere shifts, film color, the printed color of these pages as they age. For American philosopher Stanley Cavell, color's signifying function in film is threefold: aesthetic unifier, world-building strategy, and temporal index. Buday's own use of color follows cinematic precedents, and as in the work of Wim Wenders and David Lynch, constructs visual continuities that bridge time and that shape and reshape worlds. While not so consistent as the leitmotif of red-and-green saturated scenes in *Paris, Texas* or categorical as the iconic color coding of map-based markers, Buday's photographs chart recurring colors that link wildly discrepant landscapes. In part, this is an homage to ready-made color. Combinations of house paint recycle throughout the book's pages in shades such as Solar Energy and Regal Red, cast first on Jeep, tarp, and buildings against a backdrop of tree-lined mountains, and again on the facade of townhouses in a more suburban setting. Observing symmetries of color and geometry, Buday's photographs seem not to capture distinct moments or locations but rather collaged compositions of consistent elements that have been subtly transformed. The logic is that of a hall of mirrors—reflecting and distorting to produce imperfect twins. A red stucco meat market and the red roof of a McDonald's franchise both become color-field compositions against the open sky and a plain foreground. In the same photographs, the visual parallels are further pronounced by the golden rectangle of the painted sign on one facade and the boarded-up window on the other. By linking different sites and objects, Buday prompts his viewer to question their initial assumptions of the materials at hand. For example, in the photograph *Peace Token Cigarettes*, the yellow sign with the Native American figure parallels the luminous windows of the nighttime photograph that follows. Returning to the Peace Token sign, the viewer reads the flat plane as dimensional, wondering whether they might ascend *into* the billboard as young Ludovic did in Alain Berliner's *Ma Vie En Rose*.

In Cavell's writing on film, black and white is encoded with the past tense, while color marks a temporality that is in process and ongoing. Buday's photographs, however, render the jagged edge of real time, the built eclecticism entwining past and present that prompted Robert Venturi and Denise Scott Brown to remark, "Time travels fast today."[1] Robert Smithson is a reference point for Buday's own sense of the indirect path of progress. Writing on the industrial detritus in his hometown of Passaic, New Jersey, Smithson narrates a non-linear inversion of time, the creation of *"ruins in reverse,"* which *"don't fall into ruin after they are built but rather rise as ruins before they are built."*[2] Smithson recounts shooting a bridge with his Instamatic 400 and having the sense that he was "photographing a photograph."[3] Both descriptions suggest the act of creating something that is, already in the moment of its production, not present but past. Buday's unpopulated and

---

1 Robert Venturi and Denise Scott Brown, "A Significance for A&P Parking Lots, or Learning from Las Vegas" (Cambridge, Massachusetts: MIT Press, 1988), 8.
2 Robert Smithson, "A Tour of the Monuments of Passaic, New Jersey," in *Robert Smithson: The Collected Writings*, ed. Jack Flam (Berkeley: University of California Press, 1996), 72.
3 Ibid., 70.

pseudo-apocalyptic landscapes are pervaded by such anachronistic quirks and inversions in the fade of painted color and the juxtaposition of objects that date themselves. Inscribed "1 HELL OF A MAN" in green paint, one residence-cum-cenotaph glows neon orange at the roofline, counting years in the differential wear of its facade. Elsewhere, in a street-side window, a figurine of a cat leans, blue eyes crossed, over the beatific portrait of Pope Francis, who has faded, spectral in the sunlight, to milky shades of cyan.

According to Cavell, spectacle and illusion are precisely the conditions for an image that we recognize as natural; to take a candid portrait, the photographer resorts to stage direction ("Look at the birdie!") to avoid the sitter's compulsion to look into the camera lens. Buday's photographs evince a parallel truth—that reality has the striking appearance of the surreal, full of temporal and symbolic inconsistencies that we ignore every day. Case in point, one photograph sets a 1990s Buick Roadmaster alongside the swollen curvature of another vehicle at least fifty years older. At center, a sign reading "BEWARE OF DOG" subtitles equine not canine. If Buday's photographs draw our attention to the way we interpret reality, several images explicitly speak to the production of visual culture in juxtapositions of material reality and the figurative world of signs and ornament. The luminous tones of a floral-patterned curtain are echoed on the penultimate page in an otherworldly meadow of wildflowers. The pole dancing figure in the sign for The Old Time Hotel Go-Go Bar & Grill is dappled in colored light like the varicolored architecture behind it, but in pure Lynchian fashion makes a closer visual rhyme with the speared carousel horse on the opposite page. For Venturi and Scott Brown, billboards and road signs are an anti-spatial addendum to the architectures they advertise, a means of "communication over space."[4] The point unspoken by the architects is that of desire, aspiration, and fantasy. In Buday's photographs, fact and fiction are entangled in the workaday and the pedestrian, hinting at Cavell's proposal that "it is through fantasy that our conviction of the worth of reality is established; to forgo our fantasies would be to forgo our touch with the world."[5]

—Nicole Kaack

Nicole Kaack is an independent curator and writer. Kaack's writing has been published by *Whitehot Magazine*, *artcritical*, *Art Viewer*, *SFAQ / NYAQ / AQ*, *Artforum*, *The Brooklyn Rail*, *Sound American*, and *BOMB*. Kaack has organized exhibitions and programs at Small Editions, the Re: Art Show, CRUSH CURATORIAL / HESSE FLATOW, NURTUREart, Assembly Room, Hunter College, A.I.R. Gallery, and The Kitchen. Kaack is co-director of artist publication *prompt:* and independent publishing platform *Not Nothing*.

---

4 Venturi and Scott Brown, 8.
5 Stanley Cavell, "The World as a Whole: Color," in *The World Viewed: Reflections on the Ontology of Film* (Cambridge, Massachusetts: Harvard University Press, 1979), 85.

THE NEVER-ENDING SEARCH

Martin Buday's photographs keep us searching—each image is an incomplete story. In one frame, white arrows painted on the barks of trees point toward an impenetrable fog. In another, we are pressed up against a shut door, presumably someone's house, greeted only by a drawing of Jesus taped above the lock. Most photos have no people in them. Some are settings that we imagine were once lively, like picnic tables on manicured grass, arranged before brightly painted houses. Other times we are plunged into landscapes that have no beginning or end: a desert, a field of pink and yellow flowers, a placid lagoon.

Buday has compared his photos to Wim Wenders's 1984 movie *Paris, Texas*—how they both use color to create a mood. I see this too: the way saturated hues (lime greens, hot oranges, deep reds) make everything more beautiful and lonelier at once. But what immediately came to mind when Buday first mentioned *Paris, Texas* to me was the movie's opening scene, in which Travis, the protagonist, wanders the desert, an empty expanse ahead of him. "You mind telling me where you're headed to, Trav?" his brother eventually asks. "What's out there?" Travis, like us, here, is not searching for something specific, but is perhaps waiting for that something to reveal itself.

In Buday's photographs, we travel from Pennsylvania to Georgia to Colorado. It often feels like we're pausing on the side of the road, catching a moment that would have otherwise been dismissed: the orange doors of a motel blinding against the snow, the silhouette of a mermaid swimming over a baby-blue wall. There might be hard-ly any people, but we sense them silently and tenderly speaking to one another, whether through vibrant signs placed outside stores or objects on display in private windowsills, like a sculpture of a cat poking out its tongue. A pair of empty chairs on the sidewalk invites our company, as does the hotel painted like a multicolored candy cane. They are evidence of the caring and peculiar ways in which we build and decorate our environments—of how we're all just trying to get across to one another.

There is something vulnerable about Buday's subjects, as though we caught them off guard, as though they didn't intend to be seen so intently. I'm thinking of the crashed, upside-down pink car and the discarded mattress patterned with flowers; of the rusting green pole holding up the sign to a convenience store in Savannah. The more we reach toward these objects, and the longer we look, something curious happens: the sensation flips and we feel as though they are reaching toward us.

There is one collection of photos, though, that stands out: the ones featuring animals, both real and fabricated ones. There's the monumental, concrete, wide-eyed elephant stalled in a misty, empty lot, and the caramel pony looking directly at us from behind a fence on which a sign humorously warns, "Beware of the Dog." There's a sculpture of a serene unicorn that looks almost real in the black-and-white desert, and a great egret that meditates on a wooden ledge overlooking a canal. Our eyes fix on these animals. Confronted by their stoic and graceful sense of control, we feel we have found what we were looking for.

I am reminded of another movie, *The Great Beauty* (2013), by the Italian director Paolo Sorrentino. Similar to *Paris, Texas*, the aging protagonist, Jep Gambardella, aimlessly roams the streets of Rome to seek the meaning of his life. We only sense that his journey is coming to a conclusion when Jep faces, in the middle of the night, a giraffe in the ancient ruins of the Baths of Caracalla. Stunned, he takes off his hat and gazes up at the towering animal as it calmly wiggles its ears. Just a few scenes later, he is similarly amazed when dozens of flamingos materialize on his patio at dawn. In both instances, the animals disappear as suddenly as they appeared, causing a shift in our protagonist. He finds a sense of inner peace, perhaps; he is a little less restless, more aware of the remarkable beauty around him. In an interview about his film, Sorrentino described "this encounter with an animal" as "a sort of rendezvous with a truth to perhaps be found within yourself."

What is it about animals? As John Berger writes in his 1977 essay "Looking at Animals," they intrigue us for being like us, but not us. There will always be the silence held between our kind, an impenetrable mystery, which is maybe why for centuries we have resorted to animal metaphors and symbols to help explain our mystifying lives (the zodiac signs are just one of many examples Berger cites). The effect of stumbling upon Buday's photos of animals is similar to Jep's sudden encounters: they make us pause and look for that truth within ourselves—namely, that this constant, unknown search will never really end. It's what it means to live.

—Elisa Wouk Almino

Elisa Wouk Almino is a senior editor at the online art magazine *Hyperallergic,* editor of *Alice Trumbull Mason: Pioneer of American Abstraction* (Rizzoli, 2020), and translator of *This House* by Ana Martins Marques (Scrambler Books, 2017). Her essays have appeared in the *Paris Review Daily*, *Literary Hub*, *NYR Daily*, *Los Angeles Times*, and other places. She teaches literary translation at UCLA Extension and art writing at Catapult.

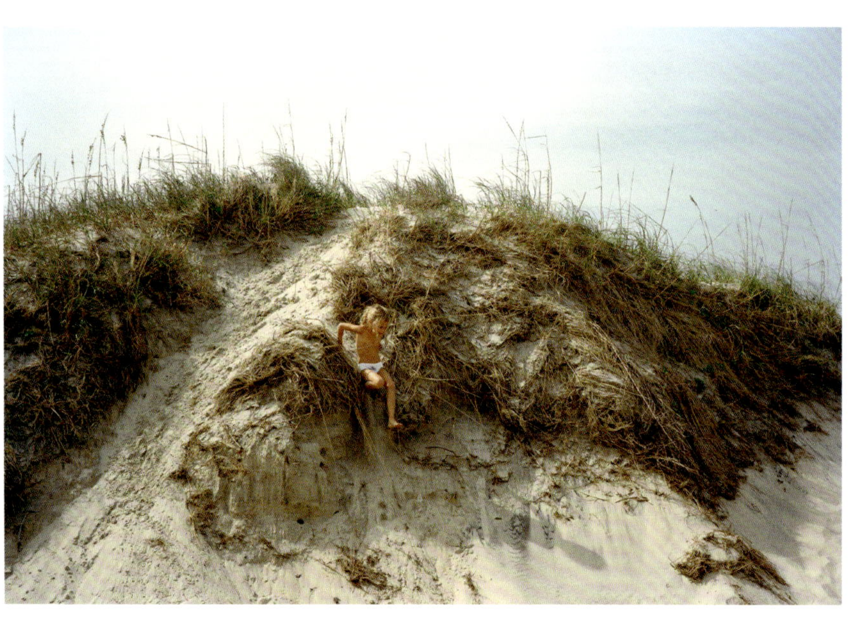

ACKNOWLEDGMENTS

This book is the result of numerous years on the road, traveling, looking, and working in solitude, but I am deeply indebted to many people who have helped bring it to fruition. It would be impossible for me to express my gratitude to everyone, but I do remember all the acts of kindness and support regarding my work. This includes a simple like or encouraging words on social media, showing my work in your gallery, printing it in a publication, sharing it with others, writing about it, purchasing a print, or processing my film. I must also give a nod to every artist that I've ever been inspired by.

Specifically, I thank my wife Erin for her saint-like patience and utmost support. I couldn't do any of this without her by my side. Keith Yahrling, master printer at the Philadelphia Photo Arts Center, for his expertise and the many years scanning my negatives, retouching, color correcting, printing, and finishing. I wouldn't trust anybody else with that job. Everyone else at PPAC for their help over the years. Ursula Damm for her kind assistance with designing these pages and the rest of Daylight Books for their professionalism and belief in realizing this project. Elisa Wouk Almino and Nicole Kaack for their generous time writing these beautiful and insightful essays. Cori Kipps, Ian McHenry and Emlyn McFarland for their talents and help with the presale.

Further, I'd like to thank all of my former professors and fellow students at the Savannah College of Art and Design for helping me initially find my voice and focus. Prior to this, Christopher Goodney for being my first darkroom pal at the Pittsburgh Filmmakers. Discovering the magic of photography together is a wonderful memory I'll cherish forever.

Finally, I humbly extend my sincere gratitude to all of my family, friends, and anyone reading these words right now. Thank you all.

(Gerry, you are dearly missed, I love you, and I wish you could see this!)